Cuddly Crochet

Adorable Toys, Hats, and More

Stacey Trock

Martingale®
& COMPANY

Acknowledgments

I was a very energetic child. My mom, no doubt anxious for a daughter who was quietly occupied, taught me to crochet when I was six years old. And look where I am! Thanks, Mom, for wanting some quiet. It worked out really well for both of us.

I am immensely grateful to Tim, who is not only amazingly caring, but is ceaselessly excited about my work. A soft ball of yarn and a Tim are the most inspiring things on Earth.

I have been delighted to work with the folks at Martingale & Company, who have taken my (admittedly cute) animals and turned them into a book of my dreams. Ursula Reikes (editor extraordinaire), Karen Soltys, Regina Girard, Brent Kane, and Tina Cook have all done wonders at various stages of the process, while also being a complete pleasure to work with. It wouldn't be a book without you guys!

And last but not least, thanks to everyone at A Tangled Skein (my LYS in Hyattsville, Maryland), where I've sit-and-stitched as well as gotten much encouragement and *ooohs* and *aaahs*. You make my Wednesday nights rock!

Dedication

To Tim, Mom and Clyde, and Dad, who are endlessly supportive of my zany ideas.

Cuddly Crochet: Adorable Toys, Hats, and More
© 2010 by Stacey Trock

Martingale®
& COMPANY

Martingale & Company
20205 144th Ave. NE
Woodinville, WA 98072-8478 USA
www.martingale-pub.com

Printed in China
15 14 13 12 11 10   8 7 6 5 4 3 2 1

Library of Congress Cataloging-in-Publication Data is available upon request.

ISBN: 978-1-56477-985-4

MISSION STATEMENT

Dedicated to providing quality products and service to inspire creativity.

CREDITS

President & CEO • Tom Wierzbicki

Editor in Chief • Mary V. Green

Managing Editor • Tina Cook

Developmental Editor • Karen Costello Soltys

Technical Editor • Ursula Reikes

Copy Editor • Liz McGehee

Design Director • Stan Green

Production Manager • Regina Girard

Illustrator • Laurel Strand

Cover & Text Designer • Regina Girard

Photographer • Brent Kane

Contents

Introduction

Welcome to my book. Since you're reading it, you probably agree with me that stuffed animals and kiddie accessories are cute. But you may not know that they're also fun to make! Whether you're a beginning crocheter or someone with years of experience under your belt, this book provides lots of adorable patterns and tips to make crocheting them a joy.

I love stuffed animals; they're cute, cuddly, and everyone from children to adults can enjoy them. But when I looked around for crocheted stuffed animal patterns (also called *amigurumi*—roughly meaning "knitted doll" in Japanese), I noticed that most patterns make tiny animals, about 2" to 3" tall. They're cute, but impractical for small children. So I started designing my own animals: full-sized stuffed animals that you can really cuddle.

This book features 10 stuffed toys, each with an accompanying project. The projects include blankets to snuggle in, hats to keep a little one's head warm, and bibs to keep kiddies clean at mealtimes. My philosophy in designing baby items is that variety is key. Some crocheters are looking for a blanket pattern made by assembling squares so that they can crochet on the go. Others despise assembling and want a blanket with miles of single crochet. Some want a blanket made with a bulky yarn so that it can be crocheted in a snap. Others are looking for an intricate design to expand their crochet abilities. No matter your style, this book contains patterns for you! And, because not all parents choose to find out the gender of their baby before birth, this book includes many unisex baby items to make gift giving a snap.

I believe that crocheting should be fun and creative—you don't have to do exactly what I do! Does your daughter love purple? Make the pig in her favorite lavender. Is your best friend having a little boy? Ditch the green and yellow in the teddy-bear blanket and crochet it up in blue and white. What you do with these patterns is up to you—as long as you enjoy them!

So, whip out your crochet hook and get stitching!
—Stacey

Getting Started

Choosing the right tools and understanding some basic guidelines will help you make the adorable toys and projects in this book. Also, understanding how yarns work will make personalizing the patterns fun and easy.

Choosing a Yarn

First of all, you don't have to use the yarns that I used. I selected the yarns I did because I liked them and I think they're well suited for the project, but there are thousands of yarns out there, so I encourage you to experiment. That said, you shouldn't use just any old yarn. So here are a few tips for successful yarn substitution.

There are three key considerations in selecting a yarn: weight, care, and fiber content. If, by the way, you haven't become acquainted with yarn labels, take a look. This is where manufacturers list information that is crucial for successful yarn substitution.

Weight refers to how thick the yarn is. In general, unless you love doing swatches and tweaking patterns, stick with the weight recommended in the pattern. Luckily, weight is often listed on the yarn label. If the pattern recommends a worsted-weight yarn, then most yarns with ⓭ on the label should be a suitable substitution. For those yarns without a weight label, refer to the "Standard Yarn Weights" chart on page 77 and look for a yarn that works up to a similar gauge.

How to care for a finished item is particularly important when choosing a yarn for baby items. It may be tempting to crochet a baby blanket out of that gorgeous, soft alpaca wool, but alpaca needs to be hand washed. In my experience, new moms running on three hours of sleep would rather throw a blanket in the washing machine than hand wash it every time the little babe spits up on it. (And, yes, your adorable crocheted creation will be on the receiving end of spit-up!) So I recommend using yarn that is washable: if the label says "handwash only," steer clear.

Washable yarns include acrylics, superwash wool (wool that has been specially processed so that it won't shrink or felt in hot water), and plant fibers, such as cotton, soy, and bamboo. I promise you'll be happy that you went the machine-washable route.

Lastly, we need to talk about fiber content. There are tons of yarns on the market made from all types of materials. In this book, I've used acrylic, acrylic blends, and cotton for items that need to be washed frequently. I used 100% wool for the stuffed animals because I like the finished product. With stuffed animals, you have a fair amount of liberty as far as yarn selection goes: the animal probably won't be washed often, and it doesn't need to keep anyone warm or cool. Feel free to substitute and pick what you'd like!

Three yarn weights (from left):
light weight, medium weight, and bulky weight

Three different fibers (from left): cotton, acrylic, and 100% wool

Crochet Hooks

There are nearly as many types of crochet hooks as there are types of yarn. There are two big factors in selecting a hook: size and composition. You're probably familiar with crochet hooks of different sizes. Bigger hooks make bigger stitches, and smaller hooks make smaller stitches. And, if you have a hook that's been made recently, then the size is usually right on your hook! So, just select the size that's called for in the pattern, or whatever your gauge tells you that you need (see "Gauge" below).

Hooks can be composed of different materials, including bamboo, metal, and plastic. Bamboo causes slightly more friction than metal, so if your stitches keep slipping around, then bamboo may be a good choice for you. If your stitches are tight and you want maximum crochet speed, then metal may be right for you. It's just a matter of personal preference.

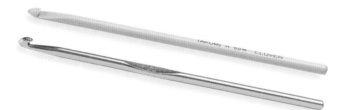

At top, bamboo hook; at bottom, aluminum hook

Gauge

You can't talk yarn without talking gauge. Each project in this book has a gauge, that is, a description of how many stitches should be in an inch using the specified yarn and hook. To check your gauge, crochet a square swatch about 6" x 6" or a small circle about 4" in diameter; then count the number of stitches you have

in that 4" to see if it's close to the gauge given for the pattern.

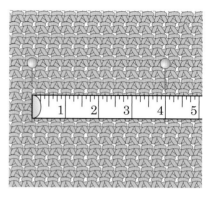

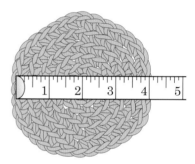

The reason for doing this is that everyone crochets differently. Some people crochet tightly, and others very loosely, resulting in different-sized stitches. If you have too many stitches in your 4", try a larger hook size; if you have too few stitches, go down a hook size.

Okay, that's the textbook explanation of gauges. Now the real question: does it matter? My answer is, not as much as many would have you believe—unless you're crocheting a garment. A too-small sweater is pretty useless. For this reason, when you make the hats in this book, take the time to check your gauge. But blankets and stuffed animals don't really need to fit anyone. So, if your gauge is a bit off (within reason), it's not too big a deal; your koala may be a half inch shorter than mine. Who's going to know? Besides, crocheting should be fun! So, by all means, if crocheting a swatch prevents you from getting started on that adorable teddy bear, then skip it!

Hat Sizing

You already know that I don't think it's a big deal if you crochet a slightly smaller or larger stuffed animal than I do. But sizing does matter when it comes to hats, so it's worth having a bit of a chat about that. The hat patterns in this book are written for three sizes: Small (newborn–6 months), Medium (6–18 months), and Large (child–small adult).

However, children's head sizes vary greatly, so it's best to avoid relying on the recommended age. For the best fit, measure the child's head and select the size that most closely matches. Notice that the finished circumference of the hat is about 1" smaller than the head circumference, because hats stretch.

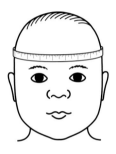

In all hat patterns, instructions are given for Small, followed by Medium and Large in parentheses, as in: sc in next 10 (12, 14) sts.

HAT SIZING			
Size	Age	Head Circumference	Hat Circumference
Small	Newborn–6 mo	16–17"	Approx 15"
Medium	6 mo–18 mo	18–19"	Approx 17½"
Large	Child–small adult	20–21"	Approx 19"

Other Supplies

While yarn and crochet hooks are the two essentials, a few other supplies are used for the projects in this book.

Animal Eyes

This book contains stuffed animals that feature safety eyes, which, excitingly, come in a wide range of colors. These eyes are made with a post on the back and are fastened with a plastic or metal washer. Commercial animal noses work exactly the same way.

To fasten these eyes, insert the post in the desired position on your animal (between two stitches), and push the washer on, over the ridges on the post. Be careful, because once you put the washer on, you won't be able to pull it off, so make sure the eye is where you want it before attaching the washer! I put both eyes in place and look at the head before fastening the washers.

While these eyes are very secure, they are not recommended for children under the age of three. So, if you're crocheting a critter for a little one this age, replace these eyes with crocheted, child-safe eyes.

CHILD-SAFE ANIMAL EYES

You can also embroider the eyes, but many people find doing so to be fussy. Just crochet these eyes in black and white yarn (in weight matching the animal) and attach. For a small animal like the bluebird, fasten off after round 1.

Eyes *(Make 2)*
Crochet through both loops.
With black, ch 2.
Rnd 1: Sc 6 in 2nd ch from hook.
 (6 sts)
Rnd 2: With white, sc 2 in each st.
 (12 sts)
Fasten off with long tail and attach to head.

Stuffing

A stuffed animal requires . . . stuffing. I use polyester fiberfill, which is readily available, inexpensive, washable, and nonallergenic (all good things!). It's available at your local craft store or fabric store by the bag. You only need a small amount for each animal, and one bag will fill many huggable toys. Different brands have different amounts of fluffiness, so it's always best to go by what feels best to you! In addition to polyester, there are a number of different stuffing fibers available, including bamboo and other fibers from renewable resources. You can even rip the stuffing from an old pillow—the best kind of recycling. While many fibers will work, I don't recommend using wool as stuffing for children, because it can be heavy and slow to dry. If your little one has a good slobber on a koala leg, you don't want the insides to stay damp for long. A machine-washable stuffing is your safest bet.

Locking Stitch Markers

Stitch markers are incredibly useful for keeping track of where you are when you're crocheting, particularly to mark the end of a round. I recommend the locking stitch markers that fasten securely onto your work. This means that it won't fall off . . . and trust me, once you've lost your place because someone was looking at your crochet and the marker fell out, you'll think it's a good choice, too.

A locking stitch marker

Tapestry Needles

Tapestry needles are used for attaching pieces to one another (like attaching the ears onto the teddy bear's head) and for embroidery. Needles come in plastic or metal and have straight or bent tips. Bent tips can make it easier to pick up stitches on the pieces that you're trying to attach. The most important thing to keep in mind when selecting your needle is that your yarn needs to fit through the eye of the needle. The tip and material you choose for your needle are a matter of personal preference.

*Top: plastic, straight needle;
bottom: metal needle with bent tip*

Keep your eyes peeled for helpful tips!

Crochet Stitches

Below you'll find an explanation of the stitches used in this book. Notice that some stitches have an abbreviation that is used in the instructions to save space. For a complete list of abbreviations used in this book, see page 76.

Slipknot

Here are two methods for making slipknots. The standard slipknot is great for all the projects, but sometimes leaves a little hole in the middle when working in the round. To avoid this hole, I teach my students to work a sloppy slipknot. Try them both and use the one you like.

Standard slipknot: The standard slipknot is easy to do and begins your work with a solid knot. To work, make a loop about 3" from the end of the yarn. Now, pull the working yarn through the loop and put the resulting loop on your hook. Pull the yarn to tighten and you're ready to start crocheting!

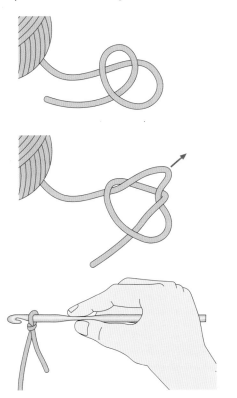

Sloppy slipknot (another option for working in the round): To work, put the yarn around your hook and simply twist the yarn once around your hook. Hold the twisted yarn below the loop on the hook with your left fingers and chain 2 stitches as written in the pattern. Then work the required single crochet or double crochet stitches into the second chain from the hook.

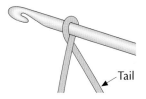

Tail

Here's the best part, once you've completed your first round, just pull the tail, and your hole closes up! Because you aren't starting with a knot, the start yarn is easily pulled shut. Hooray!

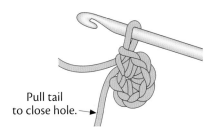

Pull tail to close hole. →

Chain (ch)

Each pattern specifies the number of chains needed to start. Start with a slipknot. To make one chain stitch, wrap the yarn over your hook. Using your hook, pull the yarn through the loop on the hook. This action pulls the new loop onto the hook and makes one chain stitch. Repeat for the required number of chains.

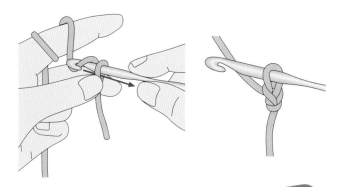

HOLDING THE HOOK

If you're having difficulty crocheting, the problem may be with how you're holding your hook. When you wrap the yarn over your hook, the front of the hook should be facing you. When it's time to pull the yarn through the loop on the hook, rotate your hook downward. This way, the hook slides easily through the loop, instead of getting caught on it.

Single Crochet (sc)

Single crochet is the stitch used most frequently in this book. It creates a thick fabric and is particularly useful in stuffed animals, because it keeps the stuffing from poking through. To work, insert your hook into the next stitch and wrap the yarn over the hook. Pull the yarn through the stitch.

There are now two loops on the hook. Wrap the yarn over your hook again and pull through both loops on the hook.

Single Crochet Decrease
(sc2tog)

Working two single crochet stitches together is a very common decrease. To work, insert your hook into the next stitch, wrap the yarn over the hook, and pull through the stitch. Insert your hook into the next stitch, wrap the yarn over the hook, and pull through the stitch—that's not a typo, do it twice! There are now three loops on your hook. Wrap the yarn over your hook again and pull through all three loops on the hook. You now have one stitch where there used to be two.

Half Double Crochet (hdc)

The half double crochet is used when you want something a little taller than a single crochet, but not as tall as a double crochet. To work, wrap the yarn over your hook, then insert the hook into the next stitch.

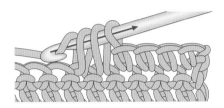

Wrap the yarn over your hook and pull through the stitch, leaving three loops on the hook. Wrap the yarn over your hook again and pull through all three loops on the hook.

Double Crochet (dc)

The double crochet is about twice as tall as a single crochet and results in a final product that is thinner and less stiff than one worked in all single crochet. To work, wrap the yarn over your hook, then insert the hook into the next stitch.

Wrap the yarn over your hook and pull through the stitch, leaving three loops on the hook. Wrap the yarn over your hook and pull through the first two loops on the hook.

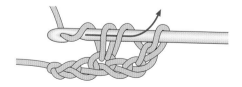

Wrap the yarn over your hook again and pull through the two remaining loops on the hook.

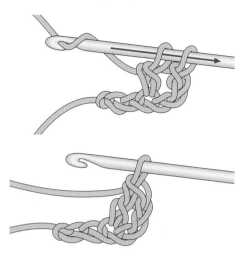

Treble Crochet

The treble crochet is about three times as tall as a single crochet. To work, wrap the yarn over your hook twice, then insert the hook into the next stitch.

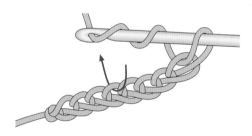

Wrap the yarn over your hook and pull through the stitch, leaving four loops on the hook. Wrap the yarn over your hook and pull through the first two loops on the hook.

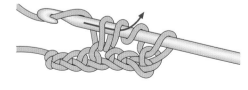

Wrap the yarn over your hook again and pull through the first two loops on the hook.

Wrap the yarn over your hook again and pull through the remaining two loops on the hook.

Loop Stitch (lp st)

The loop stitch, as its name suggests, makes a loop. This is an excellent stitch to know for making fluffy sheep or furry bits of other animals. To work, insert your hook into the next stitch, loop the yarn around the index finger of your left hand, wrap the yarn on the near side of your index finger over the hook, then catch the yarn on the far side of your index finger, and pull both yarns through the stitch.

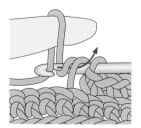

Remove your index finger and you'll see the loop! Wrap the yarn over your hook again and pull through all the loops on the hook.

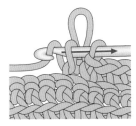

Notice that the loops form on the wrong side of your work. Therefore, when you're assembling your pieces that use the loop stitch, the wrong side with the loops will face outward.

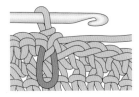

Loop Stitch Decrease (lp st2tog)

Working two loop stitches together creates a decrease. To work, *insert your hook into the next stitch, loop the yarn over your index finger, wrap the yarn on the nearside of your finger over the hook, catch the yarn on the far side of your index finger, wrap the far side of the yarn over the hook*, and pull both yarns through the stitch; repeat from * to *, now wrap the yarn over your hook and pull through all the stitches on the hook.

Slip Stitch (sl st)

The slip stitch is the simplest crochet stitch. To work, insert your hook into the next stitch and wrap the yarn over the hook. Pull the yarn through both loops on the hook.

Slip-Stitch Decrease (sl st2tog)

This decrease is used at the tip of some animal ears to create a nice pointy ear. To work, insert your hook into the next stitch, wrap the yarn over the hook, and pull through the stitch; insert your hook into the next stitch, wrap the yarn over the hook, and pull through all three loops on the hook.

Additional Techniques

The following techniques will help you crochet the projects and finish them with ease.

Working Through the Front or Back Loops

When you make a crochet stitch, you end up with two loops at the top of the stitch: a front loop and a back loop. Some designs are worked through both loops. However, in this book, most of the designs are worked into only one loop for a desired affect. The instructions will tell you which loop to work in.

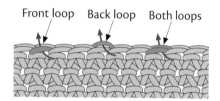

Front loop   Back loop   Both loops

Through the front loop: When working back and forth in rows, crochet through the front loops unless otherwise specified. Because working through both loops creates a thicker finished project, working through the front loop is ideal for baby items.

Through the back loop: When working in the round, crochet through the back loops unless otherwise specified. This leaves a little ridge that I think is cute. Compare the bird at left below, which has been stitched by working into the back loops, to the bird on the right, which has been stitched by working into both loops.

At left, bird crocheted through the back loop only; at right, bird crocheted through both loops

Working on Both Sides of the Chain

Some pieces are worked on both sides of the foundation chain. To do this, work the required number of chains and then work into the top loop of each chain as instructed. At the end of the row of chains and with the right side still facing you, rotate the piece clockwise so that the bottom loop of the chain is now at the top, then work into the bottom of each chain as instructed.

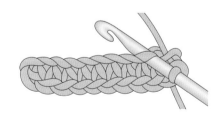

Working in the Round

Particularly when you're new to crochet, working in the round can be confusing. There is no clear indication where the round begins and ends, so it's easy to get lost. I recommend that you place a stitch marker in the last stitch at the end of the round. Then, after you've crocheted the stitches for the next round, you should end up exactly above the stitch marker. Move your stitch marker (see page 8) at the end of each round to keep track of where you are.

Follow the instructions and continue working in the round without turning until the piece is complete.

Changing Colors

When you switch from one color to another, there is a trick to doing it so the change in color is very clean. Work to last stitch before a color change (the illustration above right shows the change in single crochet). In the next stitch (the last one of your current color), stitch as usual, but do not pull the final loop through. Instead, wrap the new color of yarn around your needle and pull

that yarn through the remaining loop(s). Continue stitching with the new color.

For color changes with stitches other than the single crochet, the method is the same: do the last step of your stitch using the new color and then keep crocheting in the new color.

Weave in the tails of the two colors on the wrong side. For pieces that will be stuffed (the animals) or stretched (the hats), tie a knot with the two tails before weaving them in. The tied knot ensures that neither stuffing nor stretching over heads will weaken the join.

Fastening Off

When you're done crocheting, cut the yarn a couple of inches from your last stitch. Wrap the yarn over your hook and pull it through the last loop until the yarn end is all the way through. Tug—and you have a finished knot!

If the instructions say to "fasten off with long tail," be sure to leave about 12" of yarn before cutting the yarn and pulling it through the last loop. The long tail will be used for attaching the piece to others.

Weaving in Ends

To finish your work nicely, you'll want to weave in the ends after fastening off. To do so, thread the tail end through a tapestry needle, and weave the needle through a few stitches on the wrong side of the work. Weave about 1" so that the yarn won't come out after handling, and then snip the end so that the yarn doesn't show.

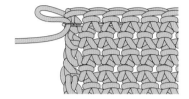

On animals that will be stuffed, you can simply knot the ends and leave the tails on the inside of the piece.

Stuffing Animals

To get a nice-looking stuffed animal, you'll need to put in a fair amount of stuffing. I always stuff the animal with slightly more than I think I'll need, because the stuffing compresses over time—especially after lots of hugs! If stuffing shows through the animal, this is a sign that your stitches are too loose, and you should go down a needle size. To avoid disappointment, you may want to test-stuff a piece to make sure it looks good before you complete the whole project!

Why do we attach the arms and legs first, and then stuff the body (instead of the other way around)? This way, when you attach an arm, you can hide all the knots (from attaching) on the inside. Then, voilá, when you stuff the animal, they're hidden! No pesky weaving in ends!

Attaching Pieces

There are two basic methods for appliquéing items to blankets and assembling arms, legs, and noses to stuffed animals and hats: 1) whipstitching pieces together using a tapestry needle and 2) crocheting pieces together using a crochet hook.

Whipstitching Pieces Together

Each pattern will tell you on what round of the body to begin attaching the arms and legs. For example, if

it says, "Attach arms beginning at round XX of body," place the bottom of the arm on this round to begin stitching. Then, stitch all the way around the arm (venturing onto other rounds of the body). For arms, the top of the arm looks best attached four rounds above where the bottom is attached, and a leg looks nice and plump when the top is attached five rounds above the bottom. Of course, these are just guidelines, so go with what you like if you can't be bothered with meticulous counting

To attach a piece to a background (such as an appliqué or body part), thread the long tail through a tapestry needle. Insert the needle through one stitch on the background piece and through the back loop of one stitch on the piece you're attaching. Continue stitching in this manner until you have completely attached your piece. See "Creating a defined neck" on facing page for specific instructions about attaching a head to a body. To finish, tie a knot and weave in the end.

Joining to background

To attach two pieces together along an edge (either to close an end that is open or to join blanket medallions), thread the long tail through a tapestry needle. With stitches aligned, insert the needle into the back loop of each piece and pull the yarn through. Repeat to end. To finish, tie a knot and weave in the end.

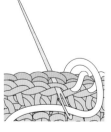

Joining pieces along an edge

Joining medallions

Creating a defined neck: The head of an animal is attached just like any other body part, with one exception. When you attach the head, pull the yarn tight before tying the finishing knot. This is going to create a neck for your animal. The bird's head (below, left) was attached just like any part, and you can see he has a bit of a thick neck. The bird on the right was made by giving the yarn a good yank after attaching the head, creating a much nicer-looking neck.

At left, bird with thick neck; at right, bird with well-defined neck

Crocheting Pieces Together

You will use single crochet to attach some parts of an animal together, and slip-stitch crochet to join strips of a blanket. To join with single crochet, place the pieces with wrong sides together and align the stitches. Using yarn indicated in the pattern, single crochet through the back loop of both pieces all around. Fasten off and weave in ends.

To join with slip-stitch crochet, place the two sides of the strips together and align the stitches. In this book, we place right sides together, resulting in the join on the wrong side. However, if you like the look of the join on the right side, you can place wrong sides together. Beginning with a slip knot, insert your hook through both loops of one stitch on each piece, wrap the yarn over the hook, and pull through all loops on the hook. Repeat until seam is complete. Fasten off and weave in ends.

Crocheting Edges

You can work in single crochet along the side of your work just as easily as you crochet in regular stitches. In this book, we use this technique to finish pieces nicely, and to switch from working in rows to working in the round. When finishing, this technique makes bumpy edges look smoother and also makes the edge easier to stitch to another piece. To crochet along an edge, join the yarn with a slip stitch into the first stitch, then just pretend that the holes along the sides are stitches, and crochet into them!

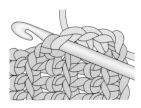

Embroidering Details

Embroidery is used as an embellishment when there just isn't a crocheted technique to suit! To embroider, thread your tapestry needle with yarn and tie a knot at the end. This knot remains on the back of the work at the beginning of your embroidery. To make a stitch, pull the needle to the front of the work, and then to the back of the work to make the stitch of the desired length.

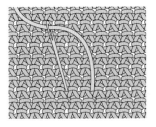

Basic Animal Shapes

Many of the stuffed animals share the same basic body parts. Instructions for the most frequently used shapes are given below. Use the yarn and hook indicated in the pattern.

Basic Sphere

This basic shape is used for the head and the body in several of the toys.

With MC, ch 2.

Rnd 1: Sc 6 in 2nd ch from hook. (6 sts)

Rnd 2: Sc 2 in each st. (12 sts)

Rnd 3: *Sc 2 in next st, sc in next st; rep from * 5 times. (18 sts)

Rnd 4: *Sc 2 in next st, sc in next 2 sts; rep from * 5 times. (24 sts)

Rnd 5: *Sc 2 in next st, sc in next 3 sts; rep from * 5 times. (30 sts)

Rnd 6: *Sc 2 in next st, sc in next 4 sts; rep from * 5 times. (36 sts)

Rnd 7: *Sc 2 in next st, sc in next 5 sts; rep from * 5 times. (42 sts)

Rnd 8: *Sc 2 in next st, sc in next 6 sts; rep from * 5 times. (48 sts)

Rnd 9: *Sc 2 in next st, sc in next 7 sts; rep from * 5 times. (54 sts)

Rnd 10: *Sc 2 in next st, sc in next 8 sts; rep from * 5 times. (60 sts)

Rnds 11–20: Sc in each st.

Rnd 21: *Sc2tog, sc in next 8 sts; rep from * 5 times. (54 sts)

Rnd 22: *Sc2tog, sc in next 7 sts; rep from * 5 times. (48 sts)

Rnd 23: *Sc2tog, sc in next 6 sts; rep from * 5 times. (42 sts)

Fasten off with long tail.

Basic Legs

With MC, ch 2.

Rnd 1: Sc 6 in 2nd ch from hook. (6 sts)

Rnd 2: Sc 2 in each st. (12 sts)

Rnd 3: *Sc 2 in next st, sc in next st; rep from * 5 times. (18 sts)

Rnd 4: *Sc 2 in next st, sc in next 2 sts; rep from * 5 times. (24 sts)

Rnds 5–12: Sc in each st.

Fasten off with long tail.

Basic Arms

With MC, ch 2.

Rnd 1: Sc 6 in 2nd ch from hook. (6 sts)

Rnd 2: Sc 2 in each st. (12 sts)

Rnd 3: *Sc 2 in next st, sc in next st; rep from * 5 times. (18 sts)

Rnds 4–11: Sc in each st.

Fasten off with long tail.

Annie the Adorable Bluebird

Annie the Bluebird is a great project to introduce you to crocheted stuffed animals—she's quick, easy, and adorable!

Skill Level: Beginner ■□□□
Size: Approx 4" tall

Gauge

5 rnds of sc = 2" diameter circle

Materials

Yarns

All yarns are worsted-weight. (**4**)

See "Featured Yarns" on page 78 for specific brands used and "Choosing a Yarn" on page 5 for substitution guidelines.

MC	40 yards, blue
A	5 yards, white
B	5 yards, yellow

Hooks and Notions

Size H-8 (5.0 mm) crochet hook

Tapestry needle

Two 12 mm black animal eyes

Stuffing

Unless otherwise instructed, work through back loops only.

Body/Head

(Make 1 body and 1 head)

With MC, ch 2.
Rnd 1: Sc 6 in 2nd ch from hook. (6 sts)
Rnd 2: Sc 2 in each st. (12 sts)

Rnd 3: *Sc 2 in next st, sc in next st; rep from * 5 times. (18 sts)

Rnd 4: *Sc 2 in next st, sc in next 2 sts; rep from * 5 times. (24 sts)

Rnd 5: *Sc 2 in next st, sc in next 3 sts; rep from * 5 times. (30 sts)

Rnds 6–10: Sc in each st.

Rnd 11: *Sc2tog, sc in next 3 sts; rep from * 5 times. (24 sts)

Rnd 12: *Sc2tog, sc in next 2 sts; rep from * 5 times. (18 sts)

Fasten off with long tail.

Feet (Make 2)

With B, ch 4.

Row 1: Dc 5 in 4th ch from hook. (ch 3 counts as 1 dc, 6 dc total)

Fasten off with long tail.

DIFFERENT COLORED BIRDS

Despite her title, Annie doesn't have to be blue! Try a red yarn to make a red bird, or yellow to make an adorable little chick!

Wings

Inner Wing (Make 2)

With A, ch 2.

Rnd 1: Sc 6 in 2nd ch from hook. (6 sts)

Rnd 2: Sc 2 in each st. (12 sts)

Rnd 3: *Sc 2 in next st, sc in next st; rep from * 5 times. (18 sts)

Fasten off.

Outer Wing (Make 2)

With MC, ch 2.

Rnd 1: Sc 6 in 2nd ch from hook. (6 sts)

Rnd 2: Sc 2 in each st. (12 sts)

Rnd 3: *Sc 2 in next st, sc in next st; rep from * 5 times. (18 sts)

Do not fasten off.

Joining Inner and Outer Wing

See "Crocheting Pieces Together" on page 17.

With WS tog and MC, sc rnd 3 of inner and outer wing tog as follows: *sc 2 in next st, sc in next 2 sts; rep from * 5 times. (24 sts)

Fasten off with long tail.

Tail

Work through front loops.

With MC, ch 7, turn.

Row 1: Sc in 2nd ch from hook and in next 5 chs. Turn. (6 sts)

Rows 2 and 3: Ch 1, sc in each st. Turn.

Row 4: Dc 4 in 3rd st from hook, dc 4 in next st, sk 1 st, sl st in last st.

Fasten off with long tail.

Beak

With B, ch 2.

Rnd 1: Sc 6 in 2nd ch from hook. (6 sts)

Rnd 2: *Sc 2 in next st, sc in next st; rep from * 2 times. (9 sts)

Fasten off with long tail.

Thread the long tail on a tapestry needle and pull through all sts on rnd 2, *going from front to back in back loop of first st, then from back to front in back loop of next st; rep from * 3 times. Pull tight to gather sts until beak resembles a cone shape.

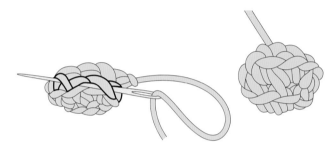

Assembly

See "Whipstitching Pieces Together" on page 16.

Attach flat side of feet to rnd 3 of body.

Attach wings to rnd 11 of body.

Fold base of tail in half and attach tail to body with fold facing down.

Attach beak to head.

Fasten eyes to head.

Stuff head and body. Using long tail from head, attach head to body, pulling tightly to form neck (see page 17).

Hoodie Bird Blanket

Worsted-weight yarn and single crochet make this blanket thick
and cozy. Children will love the hood for games of peekaboo!

Skill Level: Beginner ◼◻◻◻

Size: Approx 31" x 31"

Gauge

9 rnds in sc = 4" x 4"

Materials

Yarns

All yarns are worsted-weight. (4)

*See "Featured Yarns" on page 78 for
specific brands used and "Choosing a
Yarn" on page 5 for substitution guidelines.*

MC	1,050 yards, blue
A	60 yards, orange
B	5 yards, white
C	5 yards, black

Hooks and Notions

Size H-8 (5 mm) crochet hook

Tapestry needle

---

*Unless otherwise instructed, work through back loops
only when working in the round, and through front loops
only when working in rows.*

Blanket

With MC, ch 2.

Rnd 1: Sc 8 in 2nd ch from hook. (8 sts)

Rnd 2: *Sc 3 in next st, sc in next st; rep from * 3 times.
(16 sts)

Rnd 3: Sc in next st, *sc 3 in next st, sc in next 3 sts;
rep from * 2 times, sc 3 in next st, sc in next 2 sts.
(24 sts)

Rnd 4: Sc in next 2 sts, *sc 3 in next st, sc in next 5 sts;
rep from * 2 times, sc 3 in next st, sc in next 3 sts.
(32 sts)

Rnd 5: Sc in next 3 sts, *sc 3 in next st, sc in next 7 sts; rep from * 2 times, sc 3 in next st, sc in next 4 sts. (40 sts)

Cont working rnds in patt as established, working 3 sc in center st of each corner and 2 more sc on each side of square until blanket measures approx 30" square.

Fasten off.

COUNTING ROUNDS IN THE BLANKET

Are you tired of counting? After a couple of rounds, you'll notice that there is a hole in each of the four corners of the blanket, which is created every time you single crochet three times in the same stitch. All you need to remember to keep your square pattern is to single crochet three times into the center stitch when you see this hole. The rest of the time, you just single crochet around and around!

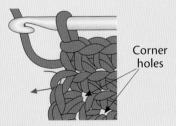

Corner holes

Birdie Hood

The hood is a triangle that will fit neatly into the corner of your blanket. The shape is created by increasing two stitches at the beg of each row.

With MC, ch 3. Turn.

Row 1: Sc in 2nd ch from hook and in next st. Turn. (2 sts)

Row 2: Ch 3, sc in 2nd ch from hook and in next ch, sc in each st across. Turn. (4 sts)

Rows 3–33: Ch 3, sc in 2nd ch from hook and in next ch, sc in each st across. Turn. (66 sts after rnd 33)

To finish hood, sc 49 along each side of diagonal (this averages 3 sts for every 2 rows). See "Crocheting Edges" on page 17.

Fasten off with long tail.

Feet

Big Foot Circle (Make 2)

With A, ch 2.

Rnd 1: Sc 6 in 2nd ch from hook. (6 sts)

Rnd 2: Sc 2 in each st. (12 sts)

Rnd 3: *Sc 2 in next st, sc in next st; rep from * 5 times. (18 sts)

Rnd 4: *Sc 2 in next st, sc in next 2 sts; rep from * 5 times. (24 sts)

Rnd 5: *Sc 2 in next st, sc in next 3 sts; rep from * 5 times. (30 sts)

Rnd 6: *Sc 2 in next st, sc in next 4 sts; rep from * 5 times. (36 sts)

Rnd 7: *Sc 2 in next st, sc in next 5 sts; rep from * 5 times. (42 sts)

Rnd 8: *Sc 2 in next st, sc in next 6 sts; rep from * 5 times. (48 sts)

Rnd 9: *Sc 2 in next st, sc in next 7 sts; rep from * 5 times. (54 sts)

Rnd 10: *Sc 2 in next st, sc in next 8 sts; rep from * 5 times. (60 sts)

Fasten off with long tail.

Toes (Make 6)

With A, ch 4. Turn.

Row 1: Dc 5 in 4th ch from hook. Turn. (ch 3 counts as 1 dc, 6 dc total)

Row 2: Ch 3 (counts as 1 dc), dc in st at base of ch 3, dc 2 in next 5 sts. (12 sts)

Fasten off with long tail.

Assemble feet: Attach flat sides of 3 toes to each foot circle as shown.

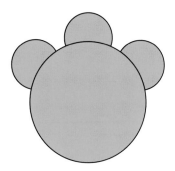

Beak

With A, ch 3. Turn.

Row 1: Sc in 2nd ch from hook and in next st. Turn. (2 sts)

Rows 2–10: Ch 2, sc in 2nd ch from hook, sc in each st. (11 sts after row 10)

To finish beak, sc 9 along each diagonal side.

Fasten off with long tail.

Eyes (Make 2)

Work through both loops.

With C, ch 2.

Rnd 1: Sc 6 in 2nd ch from hook. (6 sts)

Rnd 2: With B, sc 2 in each st. (12 sts)

Fasten off with long tail.

Assembly

See "Attaching Pieces" on page 16.

Whipstitch eyes and beak to hood.

Place WS of hood on RS of one corner of blanket with edges aligned. With RS facing you, and working through both hood and blanket, sc hood to blanket. Cont sc along rem sides of blanket until you get to beg of where hood is attached.

Whipstitch feet to blanket.

Weave in ends.

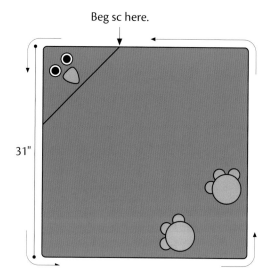

Beg sc here.

31"

Sydney the Snuggly Penguin

Snuggly Sydney may come from a chilly place, but she's
just the thing to keep your little one snug and warm!

Skill Level: Easy ◼◼◻◻

Size: Approx 7½" tall

Gauge

5 rnds in sc = 2" diameter circle

Materials

Yarns

All yarns are worsted-weight. ④

*See "Featured Yarns" on page 78 for specific
brands used and "Choosing a Yarn" on page 5
for substitution guidelines.*

MC 110 yards, black
CC 25 yards, white
A 10 yards, orange
B 5 yards, blue

Hooks and Notions

Size H-8 (5 mm) crochet hook

Tapestry needle

Two 12 mm black animal eyes

Stuffing

Unless otherwise instructed, work through back loops only.

Body

With MC, ch 2.

Rnd 1: Sc 6 in 2nd ch from hook. (6 sts)

Rnd 2: Sc 2 in each st. (12 sts)

Rnd 3: *Sc 2 in next st, sc in next st; rep from * 5 times.
(18 sts)

Rnd 4: *Sc 2 in next st, sc in next 2 sts; rep from * 5 times. (24 sts)

Rnd 5: *Sc 2 in next st, sc in next 3 sts; rep from * 5 times. (30 sts)

Rnd 6: *Sc 2 in next st, sc in next 4 sts; rep from * 5 times. (36 sts)

Rnd 7: *Sc 2 in next st, sc in next 5 sts; rep from * 5 times. (42 sts)

Rnd 8: *Sc 2 in next st, sc in next 6 sts; rep from * 5 times. (48 sts)

Rnd 9: *Sc 2 in next st, sc in next 7 sts; rep from * 5 times. (54 sts)

Rnd 10: *Sc 2 in next st, sc in next 8 sts; rep from * 5 times. (60 sts)

Rnds 11–20: With CC, sc in next 20 sts; with MC, sc in each of next 40 sts.

Rnd 21: With CC, *sc2tog, sc of next 8 sts*; rep from * to * once; with MC, rep from * to * 4 times. (54 sts)

Rnd 22: With CC, *sc2tog, sc in next 7 sts*; rep from * to * once; with MC, rep from * to * 4 times. (48 sts)

Rnd 23: With CC, *sc2tog, sc in next 6 sts*; rep from * to ** once, with MC, rep from * to * 4 times. (42 sts)

Fasten off with long tail.

Head

With MC, ch 2.

Rnd 1: Sc 6 in 2nd ch from hook. (6 sts)

Rnd 2: Sc 2 in each st. (12 sts)

Rnd 3: *Sc 2 in next st, sc in next st; rep from * 5 times. (18 sts)

Rnd 4: *Sc 2 in next st, sc in next 2 sts; rep from * 5 times. (24 sts)

Rnd 5: *Sc 2 in next st, sc in next 3 sts; rep from * 5 times. (30 sts)

Rnd 6: *Sc 2 in next st, sc in next 4 sts; rep from * 5 times. (36 sts)

Rnd 7: *Sc 2 in next st, sc in next 5 sts; rep from * 5 times. (42 sts)

Rnd 8: *Sc 2 in next st, sc in next 6 sts; rep from * 5 times. (48 sts)

Rnd 9: *Sc 2 in next st, sc in next 7 sts; rep from * 5 times. (54 sts)

Rnd 10: *Sc 2 in next st, sc in next 8 sts; rep from * 5 times. (60 sts)

Rnds 11–15: With MC, sc in each st.

Rnds 16–20: With CC, sc in next 20 sts; with MC, sc in each of next 40 sts.

Rnd 21: With CC, *sc2tog, sc in next 8 sts*; rep from * to * once; with MC, rep from * to * 4 times. (54 sts)

Rnd 22: With CC, *sc2tog, sc in next 7 sts*; rep from * to * once; with MC, rep from * to * 4 times. (48 sts)

Rnd 23: With CC, *sc2tog, sc in next 6 sts*; rep from * to * once; with MC, rep from * to * 4 times. (42 sts)

Fasten off with long tail.

Eye Circles (Make 2)

With B, ch 2.

Rnd 1: Sc 6 in 2nd ch from hook. (6 sts)

Rnd 2: Sc 2 in each st. (12 sts)

Fasten off with long tail.

Beak

With A, ch 10. Turn.

Rnd 1: Sc in 2nd ch from hook, *sc in each of next 7 sts, sc 3 times in next st*. Rotate piece clockwise and work into bottom loops of foundation ch (see page 14) as follows: sc in first ch, rep from * to * once. (22 sts)

Rnds 2 and 3: Sc in each st.

Rnd 4: *Sc in each of next 9 sts, sc2tog; rep from * once. (20 sts)

Fasten off with long tail.

> ### STUFFING TIP
>
> *If you find it difficult to keep the stuffing inside the beak while you're attaching it to the head, try this: attach the bottom half of the beak first, and then stuff the beak. This will help keep the stuffing inside while you finish sewing.*

Feet (Make 2)

Work through front loops.

With A, ch 4. Turn.

Row 1: Sc 5 times in 4th ch from hook. Turn. (ch 3 counts as 1 dc, 6 dc total)

Row 2: Ch 3 (counts as 1 dc), dc in st at base of ch 3, dc 2 in each of next 5 sts. (12 sts)

Fasten off with long tail.

Wings (Make 2)

With MC, ch 2.

Rnd 1: Sc 6 in 2nd ch from hook. (6 sts)

Rnd 2: Sc 2 in each st. (12 sts)

Rnds 3 and 4: Sc in each st.

Rnd 5: *Sc 2 in next st, sc in next st; rep from * 5 times. (18 sts)

Rnds 6–9: Sc in each st.

Rnd 10: *Sc2tog, sc in each of next 2 sts; rep from * 5 times. (12 sts)

Rnd 11: Sc in each st.

Fasten off with long tail.

Assembly

See "Whipstitching Pieces Together" on page 16.

Whipstitch the open end of wing tog.

Attach wings to side of body. Attach flat side of feet to rnd 7 of body.

Stuff beak and attach so that it straddles the color change on the head.

Attach eye circles above beak. Fasten eyes in center of eye circles.

Stuff head and body. Using long tail from head, attach head to body, pulling tightly to form neck (see page 17).

Polar Penguin Hat

This chilly little penguin won't leave you out in the cold! Keep your kiddies warm with this adorable hat, in sizes ranging from infant to child's large.

Skill Level: Easy ◼◼◻◻

Sizes: Small (Medium, Large)

Finished Circumference: Approx 16 (17½, 19)"

See page 7 for information about hat sizes.

Gauge

6 rnds in sc = 2½" diameter circle

Materials

Yarns

All yarns are worsted-weight. (4)

See "Featured Yarns" on page 78 for specific brands used and "Choosing a Yarn" on page 5 for substitution guidelines.

MC	60 (65, 65) yards, black
CC	10 yards, white
A	10 yards, orange
B	5 yards, blue

Hooks and Notions

Size H-8 (5 mm) crochet hook

Tapestry needle

Stuffing

Unless otherwise instructed, work through back loops only.

Hat

With MC, ch 2.

Rnd 1: Sc 6 in 2nd ch from hook. (6 sts)

Rnd 2: Sc 2 in each st. (12 sts)

Rnd 3: *Sc 2 in next st, sc in next st; rep from * 5 times. (18 sts)

Rnd 4: *Sc 2 in next st, sc in next 2 sts; rep from * 5 times. (24 sts)

Rnd 5: *Sc 2 in next st, sc in next 3 sts; rep from * 5 times. (30 sts)

Rnd 6: *Sc 2 in next st, sc in next 4 sts; rep from * 5 times. (36 sts)

Rnd 7: *Sc 2 in next st, sc in next 5 sts; rep from * 5 times. (42 sts)

Rnd 8: *Sc 2 in next st, sc in next 6 sts; rep from * 5 times. (48 sts)

Rnd 9: *Sc 2 in next st, sc in next 7 sts; rep from * 5 times. (54 sts)

Rnd 10: *Sc 2 in next st, sc in next 8 sts; rep from * 5 times. (60 sts)

For Small, skip to rnd 13.

Rnd 11: *Sc 2 in next st, sc in next 9 sts; rep from * 5 times. (66 sts)

For Medium, skip to rnd 13.

Rnd 12: *Sc 2 in next st, sc in next 10 sts; rep from * 5 times. (72 sts)

Rnds 13–20: Sc in each st. [60 (66, 72) sts]

Rnds 21–27: With CC, sc in next 20 (22, 24) sts. With MC, sc in next 40 (44, 48) sts. [60 (66, 72) sts]

Fasten off.

Beak

With A, ch 10. Turn.

Rnd 1: Sc in 2nd ch from hook, *sc in each of next 7 sts, sc 3 times in next st*, rotate piece clockwise and work into bottom loops of foundation chain (see page 14) as follows: sc in first ch, rep from * to * once. (22 sts)

Rnds 2 and 3: Sc in each st.

Rnd 4: *Sc in next 9 sts, sc2tog; rep from * once. (20 sts)

Fasten off with long tail.

Eyes (Make 2)

Work through both loops.

With MC, ch 2.

Rnd 1: Sc 6 in 2nd ch from hook. (6 sts)

Rnd 2: With B, sc 2 in each st. (12 sts)

Fasten off with long tail.

Assembly

See "Whipstitching Pieces Together" on page 16.

Stuff beak and attach so that it straddles the color change of the hat.

Attach eyes to hat.

Weave in ends.

> **MAKING A WARMER HAT**
>
> *Want a super-warm hat? Try a wool yarn. Not all wools are scratchy—many are super soft! Check the label for superwash wool, and you'll get a hat that can be washed just as easily as an acrylic yarn.*

Timmy the Teddy Bear

Timmy is a crocheted version of the classic teddy bear.
He is sure to please children of any age!

Skill Level: Beginner ◼☐☐☐
Size: Approx 7½" tall

Gauge

5 rnds in sc = 2" diameter circle

Materials

Yarns

All yarns are worsted-weight. (4)

See "Featured Yarns" on page 78 for specific brands used and "Choosing a Yarn" on page 5 for substitution guidelines.

MC 160 yards, brown
CC 15 yards, tan

Hooks and Notions

Size H-8 (5 mm) crochet hook

Tapestry needle

Brown animal nose

Two 12 mm blue animal eyes

Stuffing

Unless otherwise instructed, work through back loops only.

Body/Head

With MC, refer to "Basic Sphere" on page 18 to make 1 for the body and 1 for the head.

Snout

With CC, ch 2.

Rnd 1: Sc 6 in 2nd ch from hook. (6 sts)

Rnd 2: Sc 2 in each st. (12 sts)

Rnd 3: *Sc 2 in next st, sc in next st; rep from * 5 times. (18 sts)

Rnd 4: *Sc 2 in next st, sc in next 2 sts; rep from * 5 times. (24 sts)

Rnd 5: *Sc 2 in next st, sc in next 3 sts; rep from * 5 times. (30 sts)

Fasten off with long tail.

Ears (Make 2)

Work through front loops.

With CC, ch 4. Turn.

Row 1: Dc 5 times in 4th ch from hook. Turn. (ch 3 counts as 1 dc, 6 dc total)

Row 2: Ch 3 (counts as 1 dc), dc in st at base of ch 3, dc 2 in each of next 5 dc. Turn. (12 sts)

Row 3: With MC, ch 1, sc in each st.

Fasten off with long tail.

Assembly

See "Whipstitching Pieces Together" on page 16.

Stuff arms and legs. Attach legs to rnd 11 of body. Attach arms to rnd 17 of body.

Fasten nose to center of snout.

Stuff snout slightly and attach snout to head.

Attach mouth to point where snout is attached to head.

Fasten eyes to head.

Attach ears to head.

Stuff head and body. Using long tail from head, attach head to body, pulling tightly to form neck (see page 17).

Legs (Make 2)

With MC, refer to "Basic Legs" on page 18 to make legs.

Arms (Make 2)

With MC, refer to "Basic Arms" on page 18 to make arms.

Mouth

With CC, ch 4.

Dc 5 times in 4th ch from hook. (ch 3 counts as 1 dc, 6 dc total)

Fasten off with long tail.

Striped Bear Blanket

Not only is this blanket adorable, it's also suited to children
of any age. Sure to be treasured for years!

Skill Level: Experienced ■■■■

Size: Approx 44" long x 40" wide

Gauge

18 sts and 15 rows = 4" x 4" in sc

Materials

Yarns

All yarns are light worsted-weight.

*See "Featured Yarns" on page 78 for
specific brands used and "Choosing
a Yarn" on page 5 for substitution
guidelines.*

MC	1,150 yards,	yellow
CC	840 yards,	green
A	90 yards,	medium brown
B	25 yards,	light brown
C	5 yards,	dark brown

Hooks and Notions

Size H-8 (5 mm) crochet hook

4 locking stitch markers

Yarn bobbins (optional)

Tapestry needle

Unless otherwise instructed, work through front loops.

FOUNDATION CHAINS

*Note that for strips of blanket to fit together properly, it's
important that your foundation chains aren't too tight. If
you tend to be a tight crocheter, try making your foundation chains with a hook one size larger (size I in this case),
and continue crocheting with your regular size.*

Row 32: Rep row 2.

Fasten off. Weave in ends.

Teddy-Bear Strip (Make 2)

With CC, ch 176. Turn.

Row 1: Sc in 2nd ch from hook and in each ch. Turn. (175 sts)

Row 2: Ch 1, sc in each st. Turn.

Beg Teddy Bear Charts (see page 34) on next row.

Row 3: Ch 2, sc in 2nd ch from hook and in next 3 sts, pm in last st to indicate st before beg of chart. Work row 1 of right-end chart over next 27 sts, sc in next st and pm to indicate st after chart ends, sc in next 113 sts, pm in last st to indicate st before beg of second chart, work row 1 of left-end chart over next 27 sts, sc in next st and pm to indicate st after chart ends, sc in next 3 sts. (176 sts)

Cont working chart between markers at each end of strip as follows:

Rows 4–16: Ch 2, sc in 2nd ch from hook and in each st. Turn. (189 sts after row 16)

Row 17: Ch 2, sc in 2nd ch from hook and in each st to last st. Turn, leaving last st unworked. (189 sts)

Rows 18–30: Ch 1, sc to last st. Turn, leaving last st unworked. (176 sts after row 30)

Plain Strip (Make 3)

With MC, ch 176. Turn.

Row 1: Sc in 2nd ch from hook and in each ch. Turn. (175 sts)

Row 2: Ch 1, sc in each st. Turn.

Rows 3–16: Ch 2, sc in 2nd ch from hook and in each st. Turn. (189 sts after row 16)

Row 17: Ch 2, sc in 2nd ch from hook and in each st to last st. Turn, leaving last st unworked.

Rows 18–31: Ch 1, sc to last st. Turn, leaving last st unworked. (175 sts after row 31)

USING BOBBINS WITH COLOR CHANGES

The teddy-bear strip has a lot of color changes, which can be a bit complicated. There are two ways to handle multiple color changes. One, you can cut the yarn every time you switch colors. I don't like this option, because you're left with lots of annoying ends to weave in at the end. The second option is to leave the yarn uncut and continue using the yarn on the next row. But having so many strands of yarn hanging off your work can leave you with a tangled mess. A solution to this problem is to use yarn bobbins.

Yarn bobbins are cardboard (or plastic) devices meant to hold small amounts of yarn. You simply wind a small *amount of yarn on the bobbin, which keep the ends from getting tangled. If you keep your yarn tidy, then you can say goodbye to a frustrating color-work experience!*

Use yarn bobbins to keep lots of color changes tidy.

Chart ends on row 30.

Row 31: Ch 1, sc to last st. Turn, leaving last st unworked. (175 sts)

Row 32: Ch 1, sc in each st.

Fasten off.

Finishing

See "Crocheting Pieces Together" on page 17.

Arrange strips as shown and join them using sl-st crochet.

Weave in ends.

KEEPING TRACK OF YOUR CHART

The pattern instructs you to place stitch markers to keep track of where the chart begins and ends. This is really important for this pattern, because the edges contain increases, meaning that you can't always work the chart a certain number of stitches from the edge.

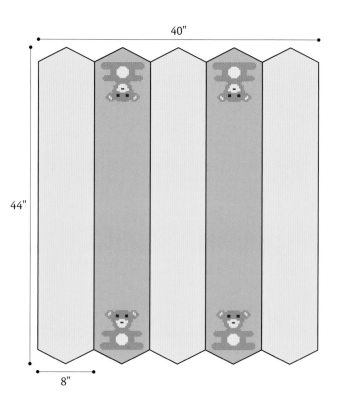

Chart for left end of strip

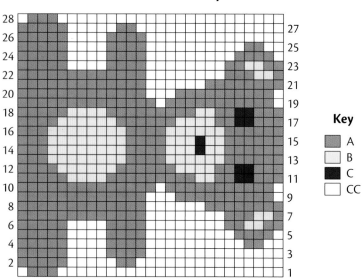

Chart for right end of strip

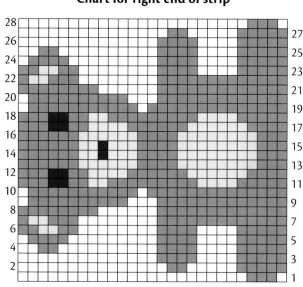

Key

- A
- B
- C
- CC

Read odd-numbered rows from right to left.
Read even-numbered rows from left to right.

Hazel the Bouncy Bunny

This bouncy bunny is sure to hop
right into your little one's arms!

Skill Level: Intermediate ◼◼◼◻

Size: Approx 9¾" tall

Gauge

5 rnds in sc = 2" diameter circle

Materials

Yarns

All yarns are worsted-weight. 🄴

*See "Featured Yarns" on page 78 for specific
brands used and "Choosing a Yarn" on page 5
for substitution guidelines.*

MC	185 yards, white
CC	15 yards, pink

Hooks and Notions

Size H-8 (5 mm) crochet hook

Tapestry needle

Two 12 mm brown animal eyes

Stuffing

Unless otherwise instructed, work through back loops only.

Body/Head

With MC, refer to "Basic Sphere" on page 18 to make 1
for the body and 1 for the head.

Legs (Make 2)

With MC, refer to "Basic Legs" on page 18 to make legs.

Arms (Make 2)

With MC, refer to "Basic Arms" on page 18 to make arms.

Cheeks (Make 2)

With MC, ch 2.

Rnd 1: Sc 6 in 2nd ch from hook. (6 sts)

Rnd 2: Sc 2 in each st. (12 sts)

Rnd 3: *Sc 2 in next st, sc in next st; rep from * 5 times. (18 sts)

Rnd 4: Sc in each st.

Fasten off with long tail.

Mouth

Work through front loops.

With MC, ch 4.

Row 1: Dc 5 times in 4th ch from hook. Turn. (ch 3 counts as 1 dc, 6 dc total)

Row 2: Ch 3 (counts as 1 dc), dc in st at base of ch 3, dc 2 in each of next 5 dc. (12 sts)

Fasten off with long tail.

Nose

With CC, ch 2.

Rnd 1: Sc 6 in 2nd ch from hook. (6 sts)

Rnd 2: Sc in each st.

Fasten off with long tail.

Ears (Make 2)

With MC, ch 2.

Rnd 1: Sc 6 in 2nd ch from hook. (6 sts).

Rnd 2: Sc 2 in each st. (12 sts)

Rnd 3: With CC, *sc 2 in next st, sc in next st*; rep from * to * once; with MC, rep from * to * 4 times. (18 sts)

Rnd 4: With CC, *sc 2 in next st, sc in next 2 sts*; rep from * to * once; with MC, rep from * to * 4 times. (24 sts)

Rnds 5–9: With CC, sc in next 8 sts; with MC, sc in next 16 sts.

Rnd 10: With CC, *sc2tog, sc in next 2 sts*; rep from * to * once; with MC, rep from * to * 4 times. (18 sts)

Rnds 11 and 12: With CC, sc in next 6 sts; with MC, sc in next 12 sts.

Rnd 13: With CC, *sc2tog, sc in next st*; rep from * to * once; with MC, rep from * to * 4 times. (12 sts)

Rnd 14: With CC, sc in next 4 sts; with MC, sc in next 8 sts.

Fasten off with long tail.

Tail

With MC, ch 2.

Rnd 1: Sc 6 in 2nd ch from hook. (6 sts)

Rnd 2: Lp st twice in each st. (12 sts)

Rnd 3: *Lp st twice in next st, lp st in next st; rep from * 5 times. (18 sts)

Fasten off with long tail.

Assembly

See "Whipstitching Pieces Together" on page 16.

Stuff arms and legs. Attach legs to rnd 11 of body. Attach arms to rnd 17 of body.

Attach tail to back of body with loops facing outward.

Stuff cheeks and attach to head.

Attach nose to head above cheeks.

Attach mouth directly below cheeks.

Fasten eyes to head.

Attach ears to head.

Stuff head and body. Using long tail from head, attach head to body, pulling tightly to form neck (see page 17).

PLACING EARS

Having trouble placing your ears? Here's a tip. Place the head (or hat) flat on a table, so it looks like a nice circle with the nose in the center. Now, attach ears along the fold, starting at the same round! It's an easy way to ensure your ears are well placed.

Bunny Rabbit Hat

Children are naturally bouncy, so they might as well have the ears to match!
This hat comes in sizes ranging from infant to a child's large.

Skill Level: Intermediate

■■■□

Sizes: Small (Medium, Large)

Finished Circumference: Approx 16 (17½, 19)"

See page 7 for information about hat sizes.

Gauge

6 rnds in sc = 2½" diameter circle

Materials

Yarns

All yarns are worsted-weight.

See "Featured Yarns" on page 78 for specific brands used and "Choosing a Yarn" on page 5 for substitution guidelines.

MC	65 (75, 80) yards, white
CC	20 yards, pink
A	5 yards, black
B	5 yards, blue

Hooks and Notions

Size H-8 (5 mm) crochet hook

Tapestry needle

Unless otherwise instructed, work through back loops only.

Hat

With MC, ch 2.

Rnd 1: Sc 6 in 2nd ch from hook. (6 sts)

Rnd 2: Sc 2 in each st. (12 sts)

Rnd 3: *Sc 2 in next st, sc in next st; rep from * 5 times. (18 sts)

Rnd 4: *Sc 2 in next st, sc in next 2 sts; rep from * 5 times. (24 sts)

Rnd 5: *Sc 2 in next st, sc in next 3 sts; rep from * 5 times. (30 sts)

Rnd 6: *Sc 2 in next st, sc in next 4 sts; rep from * 5 times. (36 sts)

Rnd 7: *Sc 2 in next st, sc in next 5 sts; rep from * 5 times. (42 sts)

Rnd 8: *Sc 2 in next st, sc in next 6 sts; rep from * 5 times. (48 sts)

Rnd 9: *Sc 2 in next st, sc in next 7 sts; rep from * 5 times. (54 sts)

Rnd 10: *Sc 2 in next st, sc in next 8 sts; rep from * 5 times. (60 sts)

For Small, skip to rnd 13.

Rnd 11: *Sc 2 in next st, sc in next 9 sts; rep from * 5 times. (66 sts)

For Medium, skip to rnd 13.

Rnd 12: *Sc 2 in next st, sc in next 10 sts; rep from * 5 times. (72 sts)

Rnds 13–25: Sc in each st. [60 (66, 72) sts]

Rnd 26: With CC, ch 2 (counts as 1 dc), dc in each rem st. [60 (66, 72) dc]

Fasten off.

Ears (Make 2)

With MC, ch 2.

Rnd 1: Sc 6 in 2nd ch from hook. (6 sts)

Rnd 2: Sc 2 in each st. (12 sts)

Rnd 3: With CC, *sc 2 in next st, sc in next st*; rep from * to * once; with MC, rep from * to * 4 times. (18 sts)

Rnd 4: With CC, *sc 2 in next st, sc in next 2 sts*; rep from * to * once; with MC, rep from * to * 4 times. (24 sts)

Rnds 5–9: With CC, sc in next 8 sts; with MC, sc in next 16 sts.

Rnd 10: With CC, *sc2tog, sc in next 2 sts*; rep from * to * once; with MC, rep from * to * 4 times. (18 sts)

Rnds 11 and 12: With CC, sc in next 6 sts; with MC, sc in next 12 sts.

Rnd 13: With CC, *sc2tog, sc in next st*; rep from * to * once; with MC, rep from * to * 4 times. (12 sts)

Rnd 14: With CC, sc in next 4 sts; with MC, sc in next 8 sts.

Fasten off with long tail.

Eyes (Make 2)

Work through both loops.

With A, ch 2.

Rnd 1: Sc 6 in 2nd ch from hook. (6 sts)

Rnd 2: With B, sc 2 in each st. (12 sts)

Fasten off with long tail.

Nose

Work through front loops.

With CC, ch 3. Turn.

Row 1: Sc in 2nd ch from hook and in next ch. Turn. (2 sts)

Rows 2 and 3: Ch 2, sc in 2nd ch from hook and in each st. (4 sts after row 3)

To finish nose, sc 5 along each diagonal side.

Fasten off with long tail.

Assembly

See "Whipstitching Pieces Together" on page 16.

Attach eyes to head. Attach ears to head.

Embroider mouth below nose as shown. See "Embroidering Details" on page 17.

Weave in ends.

Clive the Cuddly Pig

Clive is the cuddliest farm animal in town—
and, as an added bonus, he doesn't like rolling in the mud!

Skill Level: Easy ◼◼◻◻

Size: Approx 7½" tall

Gauge

5 rnds in sc = 2" diameter circle

Materials

Yarns

All yarns are worsted-weight. 🔵4️⃣

*See "Featured Yarns" on page 78
for specific brands used and
"Choosing a Yarn" on page 5
for substitution guidelines.*

MC 160 yards, pink
CC 20 yards, black

Hooks and Notions

Size H-8 (5 mm) crochet hook

Tapestry needle

Two 12 mm black animal eyes

Stuffing

Unless otherwise instructed, work through back loops only.

Body/Head

With MC, refer to "Basic Sphere" on page 18 to make 1
for the body and 1 for the head.

Legs (Make 2)

With CC, ch 2.

Rnd 1: Sc 6 in 2nd ch from hook. (6 sts)

Rnd 2: Sc 2 in each st. (12 sts)

Rnd 3: *Sc 2 in next st, sc in next st; rep from * 5 times. (18 sts)

Rnd 4: *Sc 2 in next st, sc in next 2 sts; rep from * 5 times. (24 sts)

Rnds 5 and 6: Sc in each st.

Rnds 7–12: With MC, sc in each st.

Fasten off with long tail.

Arms (Make 2)

With CC, ch 2.

Rnd 1: Sc 6 in 2nd ch from hook. (6 sts)

Rnd 2: Sc 2 in each st. (12 sts)

Rnd 3: *Sc 2 in next st, sc in next st; rep from * 5 times. (18 sts)

Rnds 4 and 5: Sc in each st.

Rnds 6–11: With MC, sc in each st.

Fasten off with long tail.

Tail

Attach MC to body with sl st, ch 13. Turn.

Sc in 2nd ch from hook and in each ch. (12 sts)

Fasten off.

If tail does not curl, crochet foundation ch with smaller hook.

Snout

With MC, ch 2.

Rnd 1: Sc 6 in 2nd ch from hook. (6 sts)

Rnd 2: Sc 2 in each st. (12 sts)

Rnd 3: *Sc 2 in next st, sc in next st; rep from * 5 times. (18 sts)

Rnd 4: *Sc 2 in next st, sc in next 2 sts; rep from * 5 times. (24 sts)

Rnds 5–9: Sc in each st.

Fasten off with long tail.

Nostrils (Make 2)

With CC, ch 2.

Sc 6 in 2nd ch from hook. (6 sts)

Fasten off with long tail.

Mouth

Work through front loops.

With MC, ch 4. Turn.

Row 1: Dc 5 times in 4th ch from hook. Turn. (ch 3 counts as 1 dc, 6 dc total)

Row 2: Ch 3 (counts as 1 dc), dc in st at base of ch 3, dc 2 in each of next 5 sts. (12 sts)

Fasten off with long tail.

Assembly

See "Whipstitching Pieces Together" on page 16.

Stuff arms and legs. Attach legs to rnd 11 of body. Attach arms to rnd 17 of body.

Attach nostrils to snout. Stuff snout slightly and attach to head.

Attach mouth to point where snout is attached to head.

Fasten eyes to head.

Attach ears to head.

Stuff head and body. Using long tail from head, attach head to body, pulling tightly to form neck (see page 17).

Ears (Make 2)

Starting with long tail of MC, ch 12.

Rnd 1: Sc in first st (beg working in rnd). Sc in each rem st. (12 sts)

Rnds 2–5: Sc in each st.

Rnd 6: *Sc in next st, sc2tog twice, sc in next st; rep from * once. (8 sts)

Rnd 7: *Sc2tog; rep from * 3 times. (4 sts)

Rnd 8: Sl st2tog twice. (2 sts)

Fasten off.

PERSONALIZING YOUR STUFFED ANIMAL

Want to make a stuffed animal extra personalized? Check out recordable voice inserts—that can record any message you wish—in your voice! (See "Resources" on page 79.) You simply record your message, and then insert when stuffing. Then, when your loved one gives the animal a squeeze, they'll get a surprise!

Swirly Pig Blanket

The three little piggies on this blanket are a reminder of a well-loved children's story and best of all, they're cute!

Skill Level: Easy ■■□□

Size: Approx 36" in diameter

Gauge

5 rnds in sc = 2" diameter circle

Materials

Yarns

All yarns are light worsted-weight.

See "Featured Yarns" on page 78 for specific brands used and "Choosing a Yarn" on page 5 for substitution guidelines.

MC	500 yards, medium brown
CC	500 yards, light brown
A	80 yards, pink
B	10 yards, black
C	5 yards, white

Hooks and Notions

Size G-6 (4 mm) crochet hook

Tapestry needle

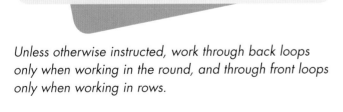

Unless otherwise instructed, work through back loops only when working in the round, and through front loops only when working in rows.

Blanket

With MC, ch 2.

Rnd 1: Sc 6 in 2nd ch from hook. (6 sts)

Rnd 2: *With MC, sc 2; with CC, sc 2; rep from * twice. (12 sts)

Rnd 4: *Sc 2 in next st, sc in next 2 sts; rep from * 5 times. (24 sts)

Rnd 5: With B, *sc 2 in next st, sc in next 3 sts; rep from * 5 times. (30 sts)

Rnd 6: With A, *sc 2 in next st, sc in next 4 sts; rep from * 5 times. (36 sts)

Rnd 7: *Sc 2 in next st, sc in next 5 sts; rep from * 5 times. (42 sts)

Rnd 8: *Sc 2 in next st, sc in next 6 sts; rep from * 5 times. (48 sts)

Rnd 9: *Sc 2 in next st, sc in next 7 sts; rep from * 5 times. (54 sts)

Rnd 10: *Sc 2 in next st, sc in next 8 sts; rep from * 5 times. (60 sts)

Rnd 11: *Sc 2 in next st, sc in next 9 sts; rep from * 5 times. (66 sts)

Fasten off with long tail.

Pig Ears (Make 6)

With A, ch 3. Turn.

Row 1: Sc in 2nd ch from hook and in next ch. Turn. (2 sts)

Rows 2–4: Ch 2, sc in 2nd ch from hook and in each st. (6 sts at end of row 4)

To finish ears, sc 8 along each diagonal side. See "Crocheted Edges" on page 17.

Pig Nostrils (Make 6)

With B, ch 2.

Sc 6 in 2nd ch from hook. (6 sts)

Fasten off with long tail.

Pig Eyes (Make 6)

Work through both loops.

With B, ch 2.

Rnd 1: Sc 6 in 2nd ch from hook. (6 sts)

Rnd 2: With C, sc 2 in each st. (12 sts)

Fasten off with long tail.

Rnd 3: *With MC, sc 2 in next st, sc in next st; with CC, sc 2 in next st, sc in next st; rep from * twice. (18 sts)

Rnd 4: *With MC, sc 2 in next st, sc in next 2 sts; with CC, sc 2 in next st, sc in next 2 sts; rep from * twice. (24 sts)

Rnd 5: *With MC, sc 2 in next st, sc in each of next 3 sts; with CC, sc 2 in next st, sc in each of next 3 sts; rep from * 3 times. (30 sts)

Cont working rnds in this manner, inc 1 st on each of the 6 sides until each side has 76 sts. (456 sts total)

Fasten off.

Pig Head (Make 3)

With A, ch 2.

Rnd 1: Sc 6 in 2nd ch from hook. (6 sts)

Rnd 2: Sc 2 in each st. (12 sts)

Rnd 3: *Sc 2 in next st, sc in next st; rep from * 5 times. (18 sts)

Assembly

See "Whipstitching Pieces Together" on page 16.

Attach nostrils, ears and eyes to pig head.

Embroider mouth below nose as shown. See "Embroidery Details" on page 17.

Attach pig heads to blanket on medium brown swirls as shown.

Weave in ends.

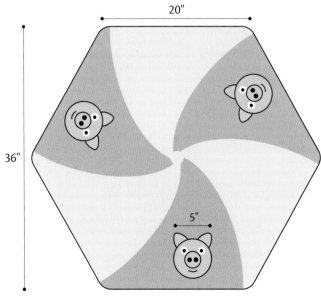

Kendra the Kitty Cat

This adorable kitty cat is sure to be loved and snuggled by all!

Skill Level: Intermediate

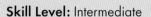

Size: Approx 8" tall

Gauge

5 rnds in sc = 2" diameter circle

Materials

Yarns

All yarns are worsted-weight. (4)

See "Featured Yarns" on page 78 for specific brands used and "Choosing a Yarn" on page 5 for substitution guidelines.

MC   185 yards, gray
CC   10 yards, pink

Hooks and Notions

Size H-8 (5 mm) crochet hook

Tapestry needle

Two 12 mm blue animal eyes

Stuffing

Unless otherwise instructed, work through back loops only.

Body/Head

With MC, refer to "Basic Sphere" on page 18 to make 1 for the body and 1 for the head.

Legs (Make 2)

With MC, refer to "Basic Legs" on page 18 to make legs.

Arms (Make 2)

With MC, refer to "Basic Arms" on page 18 to make arms.

Tail

With MC, ch 2.

Rnd 1: Sc 6 in 2nd ch from hook. (6 sts)

Rnd 2: Sc 2 in each st. (12 sts)

Rnds 3–10: Sl st in next 4 sts, sc in next 2 sts, hdc in next 4 sts, sc in next 2 sts.

Rnds 11–14: Hdc in each st.

Fasten off with long tail.

Cheeks (Make 2)

With MC, ch 2.

Rnd 1: Sc 6 times in 2nd ch from hook. (6 sts)

Rnd 2: Sc 2 in each st. (12 sts)

Rnd 3: *Sc 2 in next st, sc in next st; rep from * 5 times. (18 sts)

Rnd 4: Sc in each st.

Fasten off with long tail.

Mouth

Work through front loops.

With MC, ch 4.

Row 1: Dc 5 times in 4th ch from hook. Turn. (ch 3 counts as 1 dc, 6 dc total)

Row 2: Ch 3 (counts as 1 dc), dc in st at base of ch 3, dc 2 in each of next 5 sts. (12 sts)

Fasten off with long tail.

Nose

With CC, ch 2.

Rnd 1: Sc 6 in 2nd ch from hook. (6 sts)

Rnd 2: Sc in each st.

Fasten off with long tail.

Ears (Make 2)

Starting with long tail of MC, ch 20.

Rnd 1: Sc in first st (beg working in rnd), sc in next 11 sts; with CC, sc in next 8 sts. (20 sts)

Rnds 2–5: With MC, sc in next 12 sts; with CC, sc in next 8 sts.

Rnd 6: With MC, sc in next 4 sts, sc2tog twice, sc in next 4 sts; with CC, sc in next 2 sts, sc2tog twice, sc in next 2 sts. (16 sts)

Rnd 7: With MC, sc in next 3 sts, sc2tog twice, sc in next 3 sts; with CC, sc in next st, sc2tog twice, sc in next st. (12 sts)

Rnd 8: With MC, sc in next 2 sts, sc2tog twice, sc in next 2 sts; with CC, sc2tog twice. (8 sts)

Rnd 9: With MC, sc in next st, sc2tog twice, sc in next st; with CC, sc2tog. (5 sts)

Rnd 10: With MC, sl st2tog, sl st 1, sl st2tog. (3 sts)

Fasten off.

Assembly

See "Whipstitching Pieces Together" on page 16.

Stuff arms and legs. Attach legs to rnd 11 of body. Attach arms to rnd 17 of body.

Stuff cheeks and attach to head.

Attach nose to center above cheeks.

Attach mouth directly below cheeks.

Fasten eyes to head.

Attach ears to head.

Stuff head and body. Using long tail from head, attach head to body, pulling tightly to form neck (see page 17).

Kitty Cat Hat

Turn your little one into the cat's meow with this adorable hat.
This hat comes in sizes ranging from infant to a child's large.

Skill Level: Intermediate

◼◼◼▢

Sizes: Small (Medium, Large)

Finished Circumference: Approx 16 (17½, 19)"

See page 7 for information about hat sizes.

Gauge

6 rnds in sc = 2½" diameter circle

Materials

Yarns

All yarns are worsted-weight. 🔵4

See "Featured Yarns" on page 78 for specific brands used and "Choosing a Yarn" on page 5 for substitution guidelines.

MC	65 (75, 80) yards, gray
CC	20 yards, pink
A	5 yards, black
B	5 yards, white

Hooks and Notions

Size H-8 (5 mm) crochet hook

Tapestry needle

Stuffing

Unless otherwise instructed, work through back loops only.

Hat

With MC, ch 2.

Rnd 1: Sc 6 in 2nd ch from hook. (6 sts)

Rnd 2: Sc 2 in each st. (12 sts)

Rnd 3: *Sc 2 in next st, sc in next st; rep from * 5 times. (18 sts)

Rnd 4: *Sc 2 in next st, sc in next 2 sts; rep from * 5 times. (24 sts)

Rnd 5: *Sc 2 in next st, sc in next 3 sts; rep from * 5 times. (30 sts)

Rnd 6: *Sc 2 in next st, sc in next 4 sts; rep from * 5 times. (36 sts)

Rnd 7: *Sc 2 in next st, sc in next 5 sts; rep from * 5 times. (42 sts)

Rnd 8: *Sc 2 in next st, sc in next 6 sts; rep from * 5 times. (48 sts)

Rnd 9: *Sc 2 in next st, sc in next 7 sts; rep from * 5 times. (54 sts)

Rnd 10: *Sc 2 in next st, sc in next 8 sts; rep from * 5 times. (60 sts)

For Small, skip to rnd 13.

Rnd 11: *Sc 2 in next st, sc in next 9 sts; rep from * 5 times. (66 sts)

For Medium, skip to rnd 13.

Rnd 12: *Sc 2 in next st, sc in next 10 sts; rep from * 5 times. (72 sts)

Rnds 13–27: Sc in each st. [60 (66, 72) sts]

Fasten off.

Ears (Make 2)

Starting with long tail of MC, ch 20.

Rnd 1: With MC, sc in first st (beg working in the round), sc in next 11 sts; with CC, sc in next 8 sts. (20 sts)

Rnds 2–5: With MC, sc in next 12 sts; with CC, sc in next 8 sts.

Rnd 6: With MC, sc in next 4 sts, sc2tog twice, sc in next 4 sts; with CC, sc in next 2 sts, sc2tog twice, sc in next 2 sts. (16 sts)

Rnd 7: With MC, sc in next 3 sts, sc2tog twice, sc in next 3 sts; with CC, sc in next st, sc2tog twice, sc in next st. (12 sts)

Rnd 8: With MC, sc in next 2 sts, sc2tog twice, sc in next 2 sts; with CC, sc2tog twice. (8 sts)

Rnd 9: With MC, sc in next st, sc2tog twice, sc in next st; with CC, sc2tog. (5 sts)

Rnd 10: With MC, sl st2tog, sl st 1, sl st2tog. (3 sts)

Fasten off.

Cheeks (Make 2)

With MC, ch 2.

Rnd 1: Sc 6 in 2nd ch from hook. (6 sts)

Rnd 2: Sc 2 in each st. (12 sts)

Rnd 3: *Sc 2 in next st, sc in next st; rep from * 5 times. (18 sts)

Rnd 4: Sc in each st.

Fasten off with long tail.

Mouth

Work through front loops.

With MC, ch 4. Turn.

Row 1: Dc 5 times in 4th ch from hook. Turn. (ch 3 counts as 1 dc, 6 dc total)

Row 2: Ch 3 (counts as 1 dc), dc 1 in st at base of ch 3, dc 2 in each st across. (12 sts)

Fasten off with long tail.

Nose

With CC, ch 2.

Rnd 1: Sc 6 in 2nd ch from hook. (6 sts)

Rnd 2: Sc in each st.

Fasten off with long tail.

Eyes (Make 2)

Work through both loops.

With A, ch 2.

Rnd 1: Sc 6 in 2nd ch from hook. (6 sts)

Rnd 2: With B, sc 2 in each st. (12 sts)

Fasten off with long tail.

Assembly

See "Whipstitching Pieces Together" on page 16.

Slightly stuff cheeks and attach to hat.

Attach nose to center above cheeks.

Attach mouth below cheeks.

Attach eyes to head. Attach ears to head.

Weave in ends.

Ricky the Kutie Koala

With his curved arms, Ricky is ready-made to give your little one a hug!

Skill Level: Intermediate ◼◼◼◻

Size: Approx 7½" tall

Gauge

5 rnds in sc = 2" diameter circle

Materials

Yarns

All yarns are worsted-weight. ④

See "Featured Yarns" on page 78 for specific brands used and "Choosing a Yarn" on page 5 for substitution guidelines.

MC	140 yards, gray
CC	25 yards, white
A	5 yards, black

Hooks and Notions

Size H-8 (5 mm) crochet hook

Tapestry needle

Two 12 mm brown animal eyes

Stuffing

Unless otherwise instructed, work through back loops only when working in the round, and through front loops only when working in rows.

Body

With MC, ch 2.

Rnd 1: Sc 6 in 2nd ch from hook. (6 sts)

Rnd 2: Sc 2 in each st. (12 sts)

Rnd 3: *Sc 2 in next st, sc in next st; rep from * 5 times. (18 sts)

Rnd 4: *Sc 2 in next st, sc in next 2 sts; rep from * 5 times. (24 sts)

Rnd 5: *Sc 2 in next st, sc in next 3 sts; rep from * 5 times. (30 sts)

Rnd 6: *Sc 2 in next st, sc in next 4 sts; rep from * 5 times. (36 sts)

Rnd 7: *Sc 2 in next st, sc in next 5 sts; rep from * 5 times. (42 sts)

Rnd 8: *Sc 2 in next st, sc in next 6 sts; rep from * 5 times. (48 sts)

Rnd 9: *Sc 2 in next st, sc in next 7 sts; rep from * 5 times. (54 sts)

Rnd 10: *Sc 2 in next st, sc in next 8 sts; rep from * 5 times. (60 sts)

Rnds 11–20: With CC, sc in next 20 sts; with MC, sc in each of next 40 sts. (60 sts)

Rnd 21: With CC, *sc2tog, sc in next 8 sts*; rep from * to * once; with MC, rep from * to * 4 times. (54 sts)

Rnd 22: With CC, *sc2tog, sc in next 7 sts*; rep from * to * once; with MC, rep from * to * 4 times. (48 sts)

Rnd 23: With CC, *sc2tog, sc in next 6 sts.* Rep from * to * once; with MC, rep from * to * 4 times. (42 sts)

Fasten off with long tail.

Head

With MC, refer to "Basic Sphere" on page 18 to make 1 for the head.

Legs (Make 2)

With MC, refer to "Basic Legs" on page 18 to make legs.

Arms (Make 2)

With MC, ch 2.

Rnd 1: Sc 6 in 2nd ch from hook. (6 sts)

Rnd 2: Sc 2 in each st. (12 sts)

Rnd 3: *Sc 2 in next st, sc in next st; rep from * 5 times. (18 sts)

Rnds 4–9: Sl st in next 6 sts, sc in next 12 sts.

Rnds 10–17: Sl st in next 6 sts, sc in next 3 sts, hdc in next 6 sts, sc in next 3 sts.

Fasten off with long tail.

Nose

With A, ch 2.

Rnd 1: Sc 6 in 2nd ch from hook. (6 sts)

Rnd 2: Sc 2 in each st. (12 sts)

Rnd 3: *Sc 2 in next st, sc in next st; rep from * 5 times. (18 sts)

Rnds 4–6: *Sc in next 5 sts, hdc in next 4 sts; rep from * once.

Fasten off with long tail.

Ears

Outer Ear (Make 2)

With MC, ch 4.

Row 1: Dc 5 times in 4th ch from hook. Turn. (ch 3 counts as 1 dc, 6 dc total)

Rows 2 and 3: Ch 3 (counts as 1 dc), dc in st at base of ch 3, dc 2 in next sts. Turn. (24 sts at end of row 3)

Row 4: Ch 3 (counts as 1 dc), dc in st at base of ch 3, dc in next 3 sts, *dc 2 in next st, dc 1 in each of next 4 sts; rep from * twice, dc in last 5 sts. (28 sts)

Fasten off with long tail.

Inner Ear (Make 2)

With CC, ch 4.

Row 1: Dc 5 times in 4th ch from hook. Turn. (ch 3 counts as 1 dc, 6 dc total)

Row 2: Ch 1, work 1 lp st in next st, work 2 lp sts in each of rem sts. Turn. (11 sts)

Row 3: Ch 2, sc in 2nd ch from hook and in each st. Turn. (12 sts)

Row 4: Rep row 2. (23 sts)

Fasten off with long tail.

Assembly

See "Whipstitching Pieces Together" on page 16.

Stuff arms and legs. Attach legs to rnd 11 of body. Attach arms to rnd 17 of body.

With RS of inner ear (loops outward) facing RS of outer ear and matching sts along flat side, whipstitch row 4 of inner ear to row 3 of outer ear. Then attach ears to head.

Stuff nose and attach to head.

Fasten eyes to head.

Stuff head and body. Using long tail from head, attach head to body, pulling tightly to form neck (see page 17).

CHANGING RICKY'S ARMS

Notice how Ricky's arms are curved? Well, take the chance to position them as you'd like! Attach his arms straight out front, and he looks like he's ready for a hug (or eucalyptus tree climbing). Attach one arm pointing up, and he's giving you a wave! Have fun!

Scenic Koala Blanket

This scenic blanket features an adorable koala munching on a eucalyptus leaf.
Not only is this blanket cute, but it works up quickly thanks to double crochet.

Skill Level: Intermediate ◼◼◼◻

Size: Approx 31" x 54"

Gauge

15 sts and 8 rows = 4" x 4" in dc

Materials

Yarns

All yarns are light worsted-weight. ③

*See "Featured Yarns" on page 78 for specific
brands used and "Choosing a Yarn" on page 5
for substitution guidelines.*

MC	960 yards, blue
CC	300 yards, brown
A	100 yards, gray
B	50 yards, green
C	5 yards, black
D	5 yards, white

Hooks and Notions

Size H-8 (5 mm) crochet hook

Tapestry needle

*Unless otherwise instructed, work through back loops
only when working in the round, and through front loops
only when working in rows.*

Blanket

Ch 3 counts as 1 dc at beg of every row.

With MC, ch 202.

Row 1: Dc in 4th ch from hook and in each ch. Turn.
(3 ch counts as 1 dc, 200 dc total)

Rows 2–7: Ch 3, dc in each st. Turn.

Rows 8–17: With CC, ch 3, dc in each st. Turn.

Row 18: With MC, ch 3, dc in next 74 sts; with CC, dc
in next 15 sts; with MC, dc in rem 110 sts. Turn.

Row 19: Ch 3, dc in next 110 sts; with CC, dc in next 15 sts; with MC, dc in rem 74 sts.

Row 20: Ch 3, dc in next 72 sts; with CC, dc in next 15 sts; with MC, dc in rem 112 sts. Turn.

Row 21: Ch 3, dc in next 112 sts; with CC, dc in next 15 sts; with MC, dc in rem 72 sts. Turn.

Row 22: Ch 3, dc in next 70 sts; with CC, dc in next 15 sts; with MC, dc in rem 114 sts. Turn.

Row 23: Ch 3, dc in next 114 sts; with CC, dc in next 15 sts; with MC, dc in rem 70 sts.

Cont in this manner, working 2 less sts in MC at beg of every even-numbered row; this will move the 15 CC sts closer to top of blanket by 2 sts to create a 45°-angle branch; there will then be 2 more sts in MC at end of row. Cont until you have worked 61 rows.

Fasten off.

Leaves (Make 10)

With B, ch 19. Turn.

Sl st in 2nd ch from hook and in next ch, sc in next ch, hdc in next 2 chs, dc in next 2 chs, tr in next 4 chs, dc in next 2 chs, hdc in next 2 chs, sc in next ch, sl st in next 2 chs. Rotate piece clockwise and work into opposite side of foundation ch (see page 14); rep from * to * once.

Fasten off with long tail.

Koala Head/Body

(Make 1 body and 1 head)

With A, ch 2.

Rnd 1: Sc 6 in 2nd ch from hook. (6 sts)

Rnd 2: Sc 2 in each st. (12 sts)

Rnd 3: *Sc 2 in next st, sc in next st; rep from * 5 times. (18 sts)

Rnd 4: *Sc 2 in next st, sc in next 2 sts; rep from * 5 times. (24 sts)

Rnd 5: *Sc 2 in next st, sc in next 3 sts; rep from * 5 times. (30 sts)

Rnd 6: *Sc 2 in next st, sc in next 4 sts; rep from * 5 times. (36 sts)

Rnd 7: *Sc 2 in next st, sc in next 5 sts; rep from * 5 times. (42 sts)

Rnd 8: *Sc 2 in next st, sc in next 6 sts; rep from * 5 times. (48 sts)

Rnd 9: *Sc 2 in next st, sc in next 7 sts; rep from * 5 times. (54 sts)

Rnd 10: *Sc 2 in next st, sc in next 8 sts; rep from * 5 times. (60 sts)

Rnd 11: *Sc 2 in next st, sc in next 9 sts; rep from * 5 times. (66 sts)

Rnd 12: *Sc 2 in next st, sc in next 10 sts; rep from * 5 times. (72 sts)

Rnd 13: *Sc 2 in next st, sc in next 11 sts; rep from * 5 times. (78 sts)

Rnd 14: *Sc 2 in next st, sc in next 12 sts; rep from * 5 times. (84 sts)

Rnd 15: *Sc 2 in next st, sc in next 13 sts; rep from * 5 times. (90 sts)

Fasten off with long tail.

Koala Arm

With A, ch 23. Turn.

Row 1: Sc in 2nd ch from hook and in each st. Turn. (22 sts)

Rows 2–5: Ch 2, sc in 2nd ch from hook and in each st. Turn. (26 sts at end of row 5)

Rows 6–8: Ch 1, sc to last st, leaving last st unworked. Turn. (23 sts at end of row 8)

Fasten off with long tail.

Koala Leg

With A, ch 13. Turn.

Row 1: Sc in 2nd ch from hook and in each ch. Turn. (12 sts)

Rows 2–5: Ch 2, sc in 2nd ch from hook and in each st. Turn. (16 sts at end of row 5)

Rows 6–8: Ch 1, sc to last st, leaving last st unworked. (13 sts at end of row 8)

Fasten off with long tail.

Koala Ears (Make 2)

With D, ch 4.

Row 1: Dc 5 times in 4th ch from hook. Turn. (ch 3 counts as 1 dc, 6 dc total)

Row 2: Ch 3 (counts as 1 dc), dc in st at base of ch 3, dc 2 in each rem st. Turn. (12 sts)

Row 3: With A, ch 3 (counts as 1 dc), dc in st at base of ch 3, dc in next st, *dc 2 in next st, dc 1 in next st; rep from * 4 times. Turn. (18 sts)

Row 4: Ch 3 (counts as 1 dc), dc in st at base of ch 3, dc in next 2 sts, *dc 2 in next st, dc 1 in each of next 2 sts; rep from * 4 times. (24 sts)

Fasten off with long tail.

Koala Nose

With C, ch 2.

Rnd 1: Sc 6 in 2nd ch from hook. (6 sts)

Rnd 2: Sc 2 in each st. (12 sts)

Rnd 3: *Sc 2 in next st, sc in next st; rep from * 5 times. (18 sts)

Rnd 4: [*Hdc 2 in next st, hdc in each of next 2 sts; rep from * once, sl st in each of next 3 sts]; rep instructions in brackets once. (22 sts)

Fasten off with long tail.

Koala Eyes (Make 2)

Work through both loops.

With C, ch 2.

Rnd 1: Sc 6 in 2nd ch from hook. (6 sts)

Rnd 2: With D, sc 2 in each st. (12 sts)

Fasten off with long tail.

Assembly

See "Whipstitching Pieces Together" on page 16.

Attach nose, ears, and eyes to koala head.

Attach koala head and body to blanket body.

Attach arm and leg to koala body.

Attach leaves to blanket.

Weave in ends.

KEEPING KOALA FLAT

After you attach the koala head and body, you may find that the middle of the head and body stick out a bit from the blanket. To remedy this, also attach the head and body to the blanket at rnd 7.

29"

51"

Lacy the Lovable Mouse

◻ ◻ ◻ ◻

This little mouse has a pointy little nose
suited for sniffing out cheese!

Skill Level: Easy ◼◼◻◻

Size: Approx 8" tall

Gauge

5 rnds in sc = 2" diameter circle

Materials

Yarns

All yarns are worsted-weight. ④

*See "Featured Yarns" on page 78 for
specific brands used and "Choosing a Yarn"
on page 5 for substitution guidelines.*

MC   180 yards, gray
CC   5 yards, pink

Hooks and Notions

Size H-8 (5 mm) crochet hook

Tapestry needle

Two 12 mm brown animal eyes

Stuffing

Unless otherwise instructed, work through back loops only.

Body

With MC, refer to "Basic Sphere" on page 18 to make 1
for the body.

Legs (Make 2)

With MC, refer to "Basic Legs" on page 18 to make legs.

Arms (Make 2)

With MC, refer to "Basic Arms" on page 18 to make
arms.

Tail

With MC, ch 2.

Rnd 1: Sc 4 in 2nd ch from hook. (4 sts)

Rnd 2: Sc 2 in each st. (8 sts)

Rnds 3–20: Sc in each st.

Fasten off with long tail.

Ears

Inner Ear (Make 2)

With CC, ch 2.

Rnd 1: Sc 6 in 2nd ch from hook. (6 sts)

Rnd 2: Sc 2 in each st. (12 sts)

Rnd 3: *Sc 2 in next st, sc in next st; rep from * 5 times. (18 sts)

Rnd 4: *Sc 2 in next st, sc in next 2 sts; rep from * 5 times. (24 sts)

Fasten off.

Outer Ear (Make 2)

With MC, ch 2.

Rnd 1: Sc 6 in 2nd ch from hook. (6 sts)

Rnd 2: Sc 2 in each st. (12 sts)

Rnd 3: *Sc 2 in next st, sc in next st; rep from * 5 times. (18 sts)

Rnd 4: *Sc 2 in next st, sc in next 2 sts; rep from * 5 times. (24 sts)

Do not fasten off.

Joining Inner and Outer Ears

See "Crocheting Pieces Together" on page 17.

With WS tog and sts aligned, sc rnd 4 of inner and outer ear tog as follows: *sc 2 in next st, sc in each of next 3 sts; rep from * 4 times, leaving 4 sts unworked. (25 sts)

Fasten off with long tail.

Head

Work the head starting at the nose.

With CC, ch 2.

Rnd 1: Sc 6 in 2nd ch from hook. (6 sts)

Rnd 2: Sc 2 in each st. (12 sts)

Rnds 3 and 4: Sc in each st.

At this point, stuff nose.

Rnd 5: *Sc2tog; rep from * 5 times. (6 sts)

Rnd 6: With MC, sc 2 in each st. (12 sts)

Rnd 7: *Sc 2 in next st, sc in next st; rep from * 5 times. (18 sts)

Rnds 8 and 9: Sc in each st.

Rnd 10: *Sc 2 in next st, sc in next 2 sts; rep from * 5 times. (24 sts)

Rnd 11: Sc in each st.

Rnd 12: *Sc 2 in next st, sc in next 3 sts; rep from * 5 times. (30 sts)

Rnd 13: Sc in each st.

Rnd 14: *Sc 2 in next st, sc in next 4 sts; rep from * 5 times. (36 sts)

Rnd 15: Sc in each st.

Rnd 16: *Sc 2 in next st, sc in next 5 sts; rep from * 5 times (42 sts)

Rnd 17: Sc in each st.

Rnd 18: *Sc 2 in next st, sc in next 6 sts; rep from * 5 times. (48 sts)

Rnd 19: *Sc 2 in next st, sc in next 7 sts; rep from * 5 times. (54 sts)

Rnd 20: *Sc 2 in next st, sc in next 8 sts; rep from * 5 times. (60 sts)

Rnds 21–31: Sc in each st.

Rnd 32: *Sc2tog, sc in next 8 sts; rep from * 5 times. (54 sts)

Rnd 33: *Sc2tog, sc in next 7 sts; rep from * 5 times. (48 sts)

Rnd 34: *Sc2tog, sc in next 6 sts; rep from * 5 times. (42 sts)

Rnd 35: *Sc2tog, sc in next 5 sts; rep from * 5 times. (36 sts)

Rnd 36: *Sc2tog, sc in next 4 sts; rep from * 5 times. (30 sts)

Rnd 37: *Sc2tog, sc in next 3 sts; rep from * 5 times. (24 sts)

Add facial features:

Fasten eyes to head.

Whipstitch ears to sides on rnd 26 of head, stitching 4 unworked sts from rnd 4 of combined inner and outer ear to head.

Stuff head.

Rnd 38: *Sc2tog, sc in next 2 sts; rep from * 5 times. (18 sts)

Rnd 39: *Sc2tog, sc in next st; rep from * 5 times. (12 sts)

Rnd 40: Sc2tog 6 times. (6 sts)

Rnd 41: Sl st2tog 3 times. (3 sts)

Fasten off.

Assembly

See "Whipstitching Pieces Together" on page 16.

Stuff arms and legs. Attach legs to rnd 11 of body. Attach arms to rnd 17 of body.

Stuff body. Thread long tail through all sts on last rnd of body. Gather sts until opening is desired neck size.

Attach head to body.

Sneaky Little Mouse Bib

This adorable little mouse is looking to sneak a bite of food—
and with a messy baby, he's likely to get some!

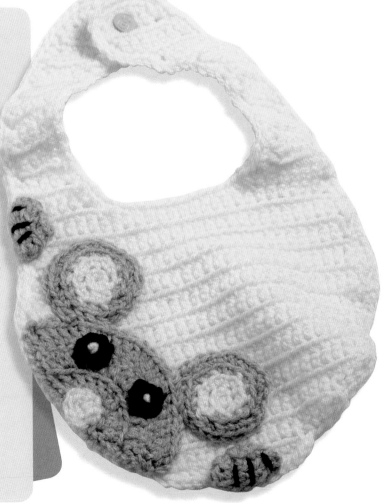

Skill Level: Intermediate ■■■□

Size: Approx 7¼" wide x 6" long (bib only);
11¼" long, including straps

Gauge

20 sts and 16 rows = 4" x 4" in sc

Materials

Yarns

All yarns are light worsted-weight. ③

*See "Featured Yarns" on page 78 for specific
brands used and "Choosing a Yarn" on page 5
for substitution guidelines.*

MC	50 yards, yellow
A	20 yards, gray
B	5 yards, pink
C	5 yards, black

Hooks and Notions

Size G crochet hook (4.0 mm)

Tapestry needle

Sewing thread and sewing needle

½" diameter button

*Unless otherwise instructed, work through back loops
only when working in the round, and through front loops
only when working in rows.*

Bib

With MC, ch 9. Turn.

Row 1: Sc in 2nd ch from hook and in each ch. Turn.
(8 sts)

Rows 2 and 3: Ch 6, sc in 2nd ch from hook and in
next 4 chs, sc in each st. Turn. (18 sts at end of
row 3)

Rows 4 and 5: Ch 4, sc in 2nd ch from hook and in
next 2 chs, sc in each st. Turn. (24 sts after row 5)

Rows 6 and 7: Ch 2, sc in 2nd ch from hook and in each st. Turn. (26 sts after row 7)

Rows 8 and 9: Ch 1, sc in each st. Turn.

Rows 10–13: Ch 2, sc in 2nd ch from hook and in each st. Turn. (30 sts after row 13)

Rows 14–16: Ch 1, sc in each st. Turn.

Rows 17–19: Ch 1, sc to last st. Turn, leaving last st unworked. (27 sts after row 19)

Rows 20 and 21: Ch 1, sc in each st. Turn.

Row 22: Ch 1, sc to last st, leaving last st unworked. (26 sts)

Fasten off.

Ties

First side: With MC and RS facing you, join with sl st 9 sts from where you fastened off.

Row 1: Sc in next 8 sts (you should be at last st). Turn. (8 sts)

Row 2: Ch 1, sc in next 6 sts. Turn, leaving last 2 sts unworked. (6 sts)

Rows 3 and 4: Ch 1, sc to last st. Turn, leaving last st unworked. (4 sts at end of row 4)

Rows 5–8: Ch 1, sc in each st. Turn.

Row 9: Ch 2, sc in 2nd ch from hook, sc in next 3 sts. Turn, leaving last st unworked. (4 sts)

Row 10: Ch 1, sc in each st. Turn.

Rows 11–14: Rep rows 9 and 10 twice. Turn.

Row 15: Ch 3, sc in 2nd ch from hook and in next ch, sc in next 3 sts. Turn, leaving last st unworked. (5 sts)

Row 16: Ch 1, sc in each st. Turn.

Row 17: Ch 4, sc in 2nd ch from hook and in next 2 chs, sc in next 4 sts. Turn, leaving last st unworked. (7 sts)

Row 18: Ch 1, sc in each st. Turn.

Row 19: Ch 1, sc in next 2 sts, ch 2, sk next 2 sts (buttonhole), sc in next 2 sts. Turn, leaving last st unworked. (6 sts)

Row 20: Ch 1, sc in each st.

Fasten off.

Second side: Turn bib over, so that WS is facing you and the side you just completed is on the right.

With MC, join yarn with a sl st 9 sts from end on left.

Follow instructions for rows 1–18 of first side above.

Row 19: Ch 1, sc in next 6 sts. Turn, leaving last st unworked. (6 sts)

Row 20: Ch 1, sc in each st.

Fasten off.

Mouse Head

With A, ch 4.

Row 1: Dc 5 times in 4th ch from hook. Turn. (ch 3 counts as 1 dc, 6 dc total)

Rows 2 and 3: Ch 3 (counts as 1 dc), dc in st at base of ch 3, (dc 2 in next st) 5 times. Turn. (24 sts at end of row 3)

Row 4: Ch 3 (counts as 1 dc), dc in st at base of ch 3, dc in each of next 4 sts, (dc 2 in next st, dc in each of next 4 sts) 3 times, dc in last 4 sts. (28 sts)

Fasten off with long tail.

Mouse Ears (Make 2)

With B, ch 2.

Rnd 1: Sc 6 in 2nd ch from hook. (6 sts)

Rnd 2: Sc 2 in each st. (12 sts)

Rnd 3: With A, *sc 2 in next st, sc in next st; rep from * 5 times. (18 sts)

Rnd 4: *Sc 2 in next st, sc in each of next 2 sts; rep from * 4 times, leaving last 3 sts unworked. (20 sts)

Fasten off with long tail.

Mouse Paws (Make 2)

With A, ch 2.

Rnd 1: Sc 6 in 2nd ch from hook. (6 sts)

Rnd 2: Sc 2 in each st. (12 sts)

Rnd 3: Sc in each st.

Fasten off with long tail.

Fold paw in half and sew the open end together (see "Whipstitching Pieces Together" on page 16).

Mouse Nose

With B, ch 2.

Sc 6 in 2nd ch from hook. (6 sts)

Fasten off with long tail.

Mouse Eyes (Make 2)

With C, ch 2.

Sc 6 in 2nd ch from hook. (6 sts)

Fasten off with long tail.

Finishing

Bib

See "Crocheting Edges" on page 17.

With MC, sc a total of 112 sts around the bib, referring to diagram for distribution of sts.

Use thread to attach button to the tie without a buttonhole.

Mouse

See "Whipstitching Pieces Together" on page 16.

Refer to photo on page 61 for mouse details.

With C, embroider 3 little lines on each paw.

Attach ears to head along 3 unworked sts of rnd 3 on ear.

Attach nose to head.

With B, make 2 pupils (see below), and attach to center of eyes. Attach eyes to head.

Attach mouse head and two paws to bib, referring to photo on page 61 for placement.

Weave in ends.

HOW TO MAKE "KNOT" PUPILS

Simple pupils are easy to make, and you don't need to embroider them! You just have to know how to make a square knot. Cut a 4" piece of desired yarn and tie a square knot in the middle of it—that's your pupil! Attach pupil to eye by simply pulling each tail of the knot through to the back, and tie a knot. Easy!

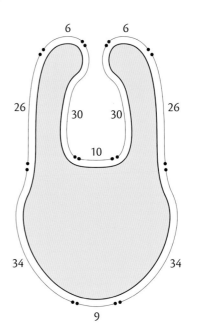

Franklin the Fluffy Sheep

You can't get any fluffier than a sheep! Franklin is made using the loop stitch, a great technique to make a super-cuddly animal.

Skill Level: Intermediate ◼◼◼◻

Size: Approx 75" tall

Gauge

5 rnds in sc = 2" diameter circle

Materials

Yarns

All yarns are worsted-weight. **4**

See "Featured Yarns" on page 78 for specific brands used and "Choosing a Yarn" on page 5 for substitution guidelines.

MC 210 yards, white
CC 10 yards, black

Hooks and Notions

Size H-8 (5 mm) crochet hook

Tapestry needle

Two 12 mm black animal eyes

One black animal nose

Stuffing

Unless otherwise instructed, work through back loops only.

Body

With MC, ch 2.

Rnd 1: Sc 6 in 2nd ch from hook. (6 sts)

Rnd 2: Sc 2 in each st. (12 sts)

Rnd 3: *Sc 2 in next st, sc in next st; rep from * 5 times. (18 sts)

Rnd 4: *Sc 2 in next st, sc in next 2 sts; rep from * 5 times. (24 sts)

Rnd 5: *Sc 2 in next st, sc in next 3 sts; rep from * 5 times. (30 sts)

Rnd 6: *Sc 2 in next st, sc in next 4 sts; rep from * 5 times. (36 sts)

Rnd 7: *Sc 2 in next st, sc in next 5 sts; rep from * 5 times. (42 sts)

Rnd 8: *Sc 2 in next st, sc in next 6 sts; rep from * 5 times. (48 sts)

Rnd 9: *Sc 2 in next st, sc in next 7 sts; rep from * 5 times. (54 sts)

Rnd 10: *Sc 2 in next st, sc in next 8 sts; rep from * 5 times. (60 sts)

Rnds 11–20: Sc in next 30 sts, lp st (see page 12) in each of next 30 sts.

Rnd 21: (Sc2tog, sc in next 8 sts) 3 times, (lp st2tog, lp st in next 8 sts) 3 times. (54 sts)

Rnd 22: (Sc2tog, sc in next 7 sts) 3 times, (lp st2tog, lp st in next 7 sts) 3 times. (48 sts)

Rnd 23: (Sc2tog, sc in next 6 sts) 3 times, (lp st2tog, lp st in next 6 sts) 3 times. (42 sts)

Fasten off with long tail.

Because loops are formed on WS of work, body will be stuffed so that WS faces outward.

Head

With MC, ch 2.

Rnd 1: Sc 6 in 2nd ch from hook. (6 sts)

Rnd 2: Lp st twice in each st. (12 sts)

Rnd 3: *Lp st twice in next st, lp st in next st; rep from * 5 times. (18 sts)

Rnd 4: *Lp st twice in next st, lp st in next 2 sts; rep from * 5 times. (24 sts)

Rnd 5: *Lp st twice in next st, lp st in next 3 sts; rep from * 5 times. (30 sts)

Rnd 6: *Lp st twice in next st, lp st in next 4 sts; rep from * 5 times. (36 sts)

Rnd 7: *Lp st twice in next st, lp st in next 5 sts; rep from * 5 times. (42 sts)

Rnd 8: *Lp st twice in next st, lp st in next 6 sts; rep from * 5 times. (48 sts)

Rnd 9: *Lp st twice in next st, lp st in next 7 sts; rep from * 5 times. (54 sts)

Rnd 10: *Lp st twice in next st, lp st in next 8 sts; rep from * 5 times. (60 sts)

Rnds 11–20: Sc in next 30 sts, lp st in next 30 sts. (60 sts)

Rnd 21: (Sc2tog, sc in next 8 sts) 3 times, (lp st2tog, lp st in next 8 sts) 3 times. (54 sts)

Rnd 22: (Sc2tog, sc in next 7 sts) 3 times, (lp st2tog, lp st in next 7 sts) 3 times. (48 sts)

Rnd 23: (Sc2tog, sc in next 6 sts) 3 times, (lp st2tog, lp st in next 6 sts) 3 times. (42 sts)

Fasten off with long tail.

Legs (Make 4)

With CC, ch 2.

Rnd 1: Sc 6 in 2nd ch from hook. (6 sts)

Rnd 2: Sc 2 in each st. (12 sts)

Rnd 3: *Sc 2 in next st, sc in next st; rep from * 5 times (18 sts)

Rnds 4 and 5: Sc in each st.

Rnds 6–11: With MC, sc in each st.

Fasten off with long tail.

Snout

With MC, ch 2.

Rnd 1: Sc 6 in 2nd ch from hook. (6 sts)

Rnd 2: Sc 2 in each st. (12 sts)

Rnd 3: *Sc 2 in next st, sc in next st; rep from * 5 times. (18 sts)

Rnds 4 and 5: Sc in each st.

Rnd 6: *Sc 2 in next st, sc in next 2 sts; rep from * 5 times. (24 sts)

Rnds 7–9: Sc in each st.

Fasten off with long tail.

Ears (Make 2)

With MC, ch 12.

Rnd 1: Sc in first st (beg to work in rnd), sc in next 5 sts, lp st in next 6 sts. (12 sts)

Rnds 2–5: Sc in next 6 sts, lp st in next 6 sts.

Rnd 6: Sc in next 2 sts, sc2tog, sc in next 2 sts, lp st in next 2 sts, lp st2tog, lp st in next 2 sts. (10 sts)

Rnd 7: Sc in next 2 sts, sc2tog, sc in next st, lp st in next st, lp st2tog, lp st in next 2 sts. (8 sts)

Rnd 8: Sc2tog twice, lp st2tog twice. (4 sts)

Rnd 9: Sl st2tog twice. (2 sts)

Fasten off.

Mouth

Work through front loops.

With MC, ch 4.

Row 1: Dc 5 times in 4th ch from hook. Turn. (ch 3 counts as 1 dc, 6 dc total)

Row 2: Ch 3 (counts as 1 dc), dc in st at base of ch 3, dc 2 in next 5 sts. (12 sts)

Fasten off with long tail.

Assembly

See "Whipstitching Pieces Together" on page 16.

Stuff legs. Attach 2 legs at rnd 11 of body and 2 legs at rnd 17 of body.

Turn snout so that WS faces outward, and fasten nose to center of snout. Stuff snout slightly and attach snout to head at center of face.

Attach mouth below point where snout is attached to head at center of face.

Fasten eyes to head.

Attach ears to head.

Stuff head and body. Using long tail from head, attach head to body, pulling tightly to form neck (see page 17).

Chunky Sheep Blanket

Bulky-weight yarn and medallions mean that this blanket crochets up quickly and is great for crocheting on the go. Plus, large medallions mean less finishing work than most medallion afghans.

Skill Level: Easy ◼◼◻◻

Size: Approx 49" x 60"

Gauge

6 rnds in sc = 4" diameter circle
    using K hook and bulky yarn

5 rnds in sc = 2" diameter circle
    using H hook and worsted yarn

Materials

Yarns

See "Featured Yarns" on page 78 for specific brands used and "Choosing a Yarn" on page 5 for substitution guidelines.

MC	1,020 yards, green	5
A	100 yards, white	5
B	50 yards, black	4

Hooks and Notions

Size K-10½ (6.5 mm) crochet hook

Size H-8 (5 mm) crochet hook

Tapestry needle

Jumbo tapestry needle (optional)

For this pattern, work through back loops only.

Plain Medallions (Make 10)

With MC and larger hook, ch 2.

Rnd 1: Sc 6 in 2nd ch from hook. (6 sts)

Rnd 2: Sc 2 in each st. (12 sts)

Rnd 3: *Sc 2 in next st, sc in next st; rep from * 5 times. (18 sts)

Rnd 4: *Sc 2 in next st, sc in next 2 sts; rep from * 5 times. (24 sts)

Rnd 5: *Sc 2 in next st, sc in next 3 sts; rep from * 5 times. (30 sts)

Rnd 6: *Sc 2 in next st, sc in next 4 sts; rep from * 5 times. (36 sts)

Rnd 7: *Sc 2 in next st, sc in next 5 sts; rep from * 5 times. (42 sts)

Rnd 8: *Sc 2 in next st, sc in next 6 sts; rep from * 5 times. (48 sts)

Rnd 9: *Sc 2 in next st, sc in next 7 sts; rep from * 5 times. (54 sts)

Rnd 10: *Sc 2 in next st, sc in next 8 sts; rep from * 5 times. (60 sts)

Rnd 11: *Sc 2 in next st, sc in next 9 sts; rep from * 5 times. (66 sts)

Rnd 12: *Sc 2 in next st, sc in next 10 sts; rep from * 5 times. (72 sts)

Rnd 13: *Sc 2 in next st, sc in next 11 sts; rep from * 5 times. (78 sts)

Rnd 14: *Sc 2 in next st, sc in next 12 sts; rep from * 5 times. (84 sts)

Rnd 15: *Sc 2 in next st, sc in next 13 sts; rep from * 5 times. (90 sts)

Rnd 16: *Sc 2 in next st, sc in next 14 sts; rep from * 5 times. (96 sts)

Rnd 17: *Sc 2 in next st, sc in next 15 sts; rep from * 5 times. (102 sts)

Rnd 18: *Sc 2 in next st, sc in next 16 sts; rep from * 5 times. (108 sts)

Rnd 19: *Sc 2 in next st, sc in next 17 sts; rep from * 5 times. (114 sts)

Rnd 20: *Sc 2 in next st, sc in next 18 sts; rep from * 5 times. (120 sts)

Fasten off with long tail (approx 24").

Sheep Medallions (Make 4)

With A and larger hook, ch 2.

Rnd 1: Sc 6 in 2nd ch from hook. (6 sts)

Rnd 2: Sc 2 in each st. (12 sts)

Rnd 3: *Sc 2 in next st, sc in next st; rep from * 5 times. (18 sts)

Rnd 4: *Sc 2 in next st, sc in next 2 sts; rep from * 5 times. (24 sts)

Rnd 5: *Sc 2 in next st, sc in next 3 sts; rep from * 5 times. (30 sts)

Rnd 6: *Sc 2 in next st, sc in next 4 sts; rep from * 5 times. (36 sts)

Rnd 7: *Sc 2 in next st, sc in next 5 sts; rep from * 5 times. (42 sts)

Rnd 8: *Sc 2 in next st, sc in next 6 sts; rep from * 5 times. (48 sts)

Rnd 9: *Sc 2 in next st, sc in next 7 sts; rep from * 5 times. (54 sts)

Rnd 10: *Sc 2 in next st, sc in next 8 sts; rep from * 5 times. (60 sts)

Rnd 11: With MC, *sc 2 in next st, sc in next 9 sts; rep from * 5 times. (66 sts)

Rnds 12–20: Follow instructions for rnds 12–20 for plain medallions.

Fasten off with long tail (approx 24").

Sheep Head (Make 4)

With B and smaller hook, ch 2.

Rnd 1: Sc 6 in 2nd ch from hook. (6 sts)

Rnd 2: Sc 2 in each st. (12 sts)

Rnd 3: Sc in each st.

Rnd 4: *Sc 2 in next st, sc in next st; rep from * 5 times. (18 sts)

Rnd 5: Sc in each st.

Rnd 6: *Sc 2 in next st, sc in next 2 sts; rep from * 5 times. (24 sts)

Rnds 7–11: Sc in each st.

Rnd 12: *Sc2tog, sc in next 2 sts; rep from * 5 times. (18 sts)

Rnd 13: *Sc2tog, sc in next st; rep from * 5 times. (12 sts)

Fasten off with long tail.

Sheep Ears (Make 8)

With B and smaller hook, ch 7. Turn.

Dc in 4th ch from hook and in next 4 chs. (ch 3 counts as 1 dc, 5 dc total)

Fasten off with long tail.

Finishing

See "Whipstitching Pieces Together" on page 16.

Sheep Head

With long tail from head, whipstitch top of head closed.

With A, make 8 pupils (see page 63) and attach 2 pupils to head for eyes.

Attach 2 ears to each head.

Using long tail of head, attach sheep head to center of sheep medallion as shown.

Assembling Medallions

Arrange medallions as shown and whipstitch tog using long tail.

Weave in ends.

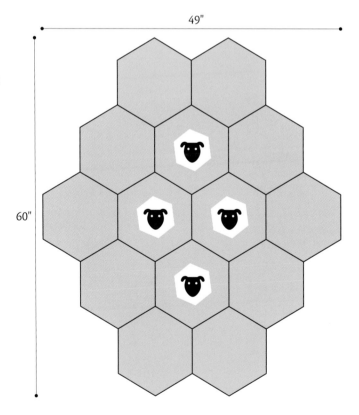

Pete the Plush Pickup Truck

This plush pickup truck is sure to zoom its way into any little one's heart!
Working in the front and back loops gives this truck its cool rectangular shape.

Skill Level: Intermediate ◼◼◼◻

Size: Approx 7" long x 4" wide x 3½" tall

Gauge

10 sts and 8 rows = 2" x 2" in sc

Materials

Yarns

All yarns are worsted-weight. (4)

See "Featured Yarns" on page 78 for specific brands used and "Choosing a Yarn" on page 5 for substitution guidelines.

MC	70 yards,	red
A	70 yards,	black
B	5 yards,	yellow
C	5 yards,	gray

Hooks and Notions

Size H-8 (5 mm)
    crochet hook

Tapestry needle

Stuffing

The unique rectangular shape of the truck is formed by alternately working in the front and back loops, so pay careful attention to which loop needs to be worked.

Truck Body

Bottom of Truck

Bottom is worked in rows.

With MC, ch 25. Turn.

Row 1: Sc in 2nd ch from hook and in each ch. Turn. (24 sts)

Rows 2–10: Ch 1, sc in fl of each st. (24 sts)

Do not fasten off.

Sides of Truck

Sides of truck are worked in the round. See "Crocheting Edges" on page 17.

Rnd 1: With MC, sc in next 11 sts (this makes first short side), sc in next 24 sts (this makes first long side), sc in next 11 sts (this makes second short side), sc in next 24 sts (this makes second long side). (70 sts)

Rnds 2–7: *Sc in fl of next st, sc in bl of next 9 sts, sc in fl of next st, sc in bl of next 24 sts; rep from * once. (70 sts)

Do not fasten off.

Cab

Cont working in the round.

Rnd 8: Sc in fl of next st, sc in bl of next 9 sts, sc in fl of next st, sc in bl of next 8 sts, sc in fl of next st, ch 9, sl st in fl of next st on other long side (joining chain across truck), sc in bl of next 8 sts. (38 sts)

Rnd 9: *Sc in fl of next st, sc in bl of next 9 sts, sc in fl of next st, sc in bl of next 8 sts; rep from * once.

Rnds 10–12: *Sc in fl of next st, sc in bl of next st; with C, sc in bl of next 7 sts; with MC, sc in bl of next st, sc in fl of next st, sc in bl of next st; with C, sc in bl of next 6 sts; with MC, sc in bl of next st; rep from * once.

Rnd 13: Rep rnd 9.

Do not fasten off.

Top of Cab

Top of cab is worked in rows.

Row 1: Sc in fl of next st, sc in bl of next 9 sts, sc in fl of next st. Turn. (11 sts)

Rows 2–10: Ch 1, sc in fl of each st.

Fasten off with long tail.

Bed of Truck

Bottom of Bed

Bottom of bed is worked in rows.

With A, ch 15. Turn.

Row 1: Sc in 2nd ch from hook and in each ch. Turn. (14 sts)

Rows 2–9: Ch 1, sc in fl of each st.

Do not fasten off.

Sides of Bed

Sides of bed are worked in the rnd.

Rnd 1: Sc in next 8 sts (this makes first short side), sc in next 14 sts (this makes first long side), sc in next 8 sts (this makes second short side), sc in next 14 sts (this makes second long side). (44 sts)

Rnds 2–6: *Sc in fl of next st, sc in bl of next 6 sts, sc in fl of next st, sc in bl of next 14 sts; rep from * once.

Fasten off with long tail.

Front of Truck

Bottom of Front

Bottom is worked in rows.

With MC, ch 10. Turn.

Row 1: Sc in 2nd ch from hook and in each ch. Turn. (9 sts)

Rows 2–5: Ch 1, sc in fl of each st.

Do not fasten off.

Sides of Front

Sides of front are worked in the round.

Rnd 1: Sc in next 6 sts (this makes first short side), sc in next 9 sts (this makes first long side), sc in next 6 sts (this makes second short side), sc in next 9 sts (this makes second long side). (30 sts)

Rnds 2–4: *Sc in fl of next st, sc in bl of next 4 sts, sc in fl of next st, sc in bl of next 9 sts; rep from * once.

Fasten off with long tail.

Headlights (Make 2)

With B, ch 2.

Rnd 1: Sc 6 in 2nd ch from hook. (6 sts)

Rnd 2: Sc 2 in bl of each st. (12 sts)

Fasten off with long tail.

Wheels (Make 4)

Work through back loops.

With A, ch 2.

Rnd 1: Sc 6 in 2nd ch from hook. (6 sts)

Rnd 2: Sc 2 in each st. (12 sts)

Rnd 3: *Sc 2 in next st, sc in next st; rep from * 5 times. (18 sts)

Rnds 4 and 5: Sc in each st.

Rnd 6: *Sc2tog, sc in next st; rep from * 5 times. (12 sts)

Fasten off with long tail.

Assembly

See "Whipstitching Pieces Together" on page 16.

For the pieces in this patt, the side with ridges showing (where you crocheted in fl for corners) is RS of work. Place bed inside back of truck so that RS of bed touches WS of back of truck, matching corners. Using tapestry needle and tail on bed of truck, attach bed to truck.

Attach headlights to front of truck.

Stuff front of truck and attach to lower front of truck.

Stuff wheels and attach to truck body.

Stuff cab and attach top to cab.

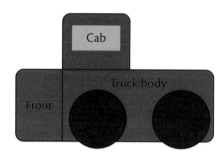

Side view

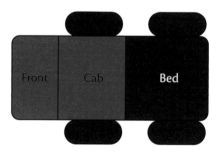

Top view

On the Road Pickup Bib

This cool pickup truck will make keeping clean at mealtime a joy for any little one, and acrylic yarn means this bib is washable (a joy for mom!).

Skill Level: Intermediate ◼◼◼◻

Size: Approx 7½" x 6" (bib only); 11¼" long, including straps

Gauge

20 sts and 16 rows = 4" x 4" in sc

Materials

Yarns

All yarns are light worsted-weight. **3**

See "Featured Yarns" on page 78 for specific brands used and "Choosing a Yarn" on page 5 for substitution guidelines.

A	15 yards,	green
B	15 yards,	gray
C	15 yards,	blue
D	15 yards,	white
E	10 yards,	red
F	5 yards,	black
G	5 yards,	yellow

Hooks and Notions

Size G-6 (4 mm) crochet hook

Tapestry needle

½" diameter button

Sewing needle and thread to match button

Unless otherwise instructed, work through front loops only.

Bib

With A, ch 9. Turn.

Row 1: Sc in 2nd ch from hook and in each ch. Turn. (8 sts)

Rows 2 and 3: Ch 6, sc in 2nd ch from hook and in next 4 chs, sc in each st. Turn. (18 sts at end of row 3)

Rows 4 and 5: Ch 4, sc in 2nd ch from hook and in next 2 chs, sc in each st. Turn. (24 sts after row 5)

Rows 6 and 7: Ch 2, sc in 2nd ch from hook, sc in each st. Turn. (26 sts after row 7)

Row 8: Ch 1, sc in each st. Turn.

Row 9: With B, ch 1, sc in each st. Turn.

Rows 10–13: Ch 2, sc in 2nd ch from hook, sc in each st. Turn. (30 sts after row 13)

Rows 14–16: Ch 1, sc in each st. Turn.

Rows 17–19: With C, ch 1, sc to last st. Turn, leaving last st unworked. (27 sts after row 19)

Rows 20 and 21: Ch 1, sc in each st. Turn.

Row 22: Ch 1, sc to last st. Turn, leaving last st unworked. (26 sts)

Fasten off.

Ties

First side: Cont with C and RS facing you, join with sl st 9 sts from where you fastened off.

Row 1: Sc in next 8 sts (you should now be at last st). Turn. (8 sts)

Row 2: Ch 1, sc in next 6 sts. Turn, leaving last 2 sts unworked. (6 sts)

Rows 3 and 4: Ch 1, sc to last st. Turn, leaving last st unworked. (4 sts at end of row 4)

Row 5: Ch 1, sc in each st. Turn.

Rows 6–8: With D, ch 1, sc in each st. Turn.

Row 9: Ch 2, sc in 2nd ch from hook, sc in next 3 sts. Turn, leaving last st unworked. (4 sts)

Row 10: Ch 1, sc in each st. Turn.

Rows 11–14: Rep rows 9 and 10 twice. Turn.

Row 15: Ch 3, sc in 2nd ch from hook and in next ch, sc in next 3 sts. Turn, leaving last st unworked. (5 sts)

Row 16: Ch 1, sc in each st. Turn.

Row 17: Ch 4, sc in 2nd ch from hook and in next 2 chs, sc in next 4 sts. Turn, leaving last st unworked. (7 sts)

Row 18: Ch 1, sc in each st. Turn.

Row 19: Ch 1, sc in next 2 sts, ch 2, sk next 2 sts (buttonhole), sc in next 2 sts. Turn, leaving last st unworked. (6 sts)

Row 20: Ch 1, sc in each st.

Fasten off.

Second side: Turn bib over, so that WS is facing you and the side you just completed is on the right.

Cont with C, join yarn with a sl st 9 sts from end on left.

Follow instructions for rows 1–18 of first side above.

Row 19: Ch 1, sc in next 6 sts. Turn, leaving last st unworked. (6 sts)

Row 20: Ch 1, sc in each st.

Fasten off.

Truck Body

With E, ch 19. Turn.

Row 1: Sc in 2nd ch from hook and in each ch. Turn. (18 sts)

Rows 2–4: Ch 1, sc in each st. Turn.

Row 5: Ch 1, sc in next 8 sts. Turn, leaving rem 10 sts unworked. (8 sts)

Row 6: Ch 1, sc in next 6 sts. Turn, leaving last 2 sts unworked. (6 sts)

Rows 7 and 8: Ch 1, sc in next 2 sts; with B, sc in next 2 sts; with E, sc in next 2 sts. Turn.

Row 9: Ch 1, sc in each st.

Fasten off with long tail.

Truck Wheels (Make 2)

Work through back loops.

With F, ch 2.

Rnd 1: Sc 6 in 2nd ch from hook. (6 sts)

Rnd 2: Sc 2 in each st. (12 sts)

Fasten off with long tail.

Truck Headlight

With G, ch 2.

Sc 6 in 2nd ch from hook. (6 sts)

Fasten off with long tail.

Finishing

Bib

See "Crocheting Edges" on page 17.

With A, sc a total of 112 sts around edge of bib, referring to diagram for distribution of sts.

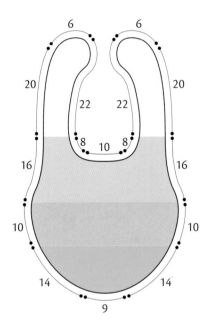

Using sewing needle and thread, attach button to tie without a buttonhole.

Truck

See "Whipstitching Pieces Together" on page 16.

Refer to photo on page 73 for truck placement.

Attach body of truck to center of bib.

Attach headlight to front.

Attach wheels to bottom of truck.

Weave in ends.

Abbreviations and Glossary

approx	approximately		**oz**	ounce(s)
beg	begin(ning)		**patt**	pattern(s)
bl	back loop(s)		**pm**	place marker
CC	contrasting color		**rem**	remain(ing)(s)
ch(s)	chain(s) or chain stitch(es)		**rep(s)**	repeat(s)
cont	continue (ing)(s)		**rnd(s)**	round(s)
dc	double crochet(s)		**RS**	right side
dec	decrease(ing)(s)		**sc**	single crochet(s)
fl	front loop(s)		**sc2tog**	single crochet next 2 stitches together—1 stitch decreased (see page 11)
g	gram(s)		**sk**	skip
hdc	half double crochet(s)		**sl st(s)**	slip stitch(es)
inc	increase(ing)(s)		**sl st2tog**	slip stitch next 2 stitches together—1 stitch decreased (see page 13)
lp(s)	loop(s)			
lp st2tog	loop stitch next 2 stitches together—1 stitch decreased (see page 13)		**st(s)**	stitch(es)
m	meter(s)		**tog**	together
MC	main color		**tr**	treble crochet(s)
mm	millimeter(s)		**WS**	wrong side
			yd(s)	yard(s)

Useful Information

STANDARD YARN WEIGHTS						
Yarn-Weight Symbol and Category Name	**1** Super Fine	**2** Fine	**3** Light	**4** Medium	**5** Bulky	**6** Super Bulky
Types of Yarn in Category	Sock, Finger-ing, Baby	Sport, Baby	DK, Light Worsted	Worsted, Afghan, Aran	Chunky, Craft, Rug	Bulky, Roving
Crochet Gauge* Range in Single Crochet to 4"	21 to 32 sts	16 to 20 sts	12 to 17 sts	11 to 14 sts	8 to 11 sts	5 to 9 sts
Recommended Hook in Metric Size Range	2.25 to 3.5 mm	3.5 to 4.5 mm	4.5 to 5.5 mm	5.5 to 6.5 mm	6.5 to 9 mm	9 mm and larger
Recommended Hook in U.S. Size Range	B-1 to E-4	E-4 to 7	7 to I-9	I-9 to K-10 1/2	K-10 1/2 to M-13	M-13 and larger

*These are guidelines only. The above reflect the most commonly used gauges and needle or hook sizes for specific yarn categories.

Skill Levels

◼◻◻◻ **Beginner:** Projects for first-time crocheters using basic stitches; minimal shaping.

◼◼◻◻ **Easy:** Projects using yarn with basic stitches, repetitive stitch patterns, simple color changes, and simple shaping and finishing.

◼◼◼◻ **Intermediate:** Projects using a variety of techniques, such as basic lace patterns or color patterns; midlevel shaping and finishing.

◼◼◼◼ **Experienced:** Projects with intricate stitch patterns, techniques, and dimension, such as nonrepeating patterns, multicolor techniques, fine threads, small hooks, detailed shaping, and refined finishing.

Metric Conversions

m	=	yds	x	0.9144
yds	=	m	x	1.0936
g	=	oz	x	28.35
oz	=	g	x	0.0352

Featured Yarns

The following yarns were used in each of the projects. See "Resources" on facing page for yardage information.

Annie the Adorable Bluebird
MC: Ella Rae Classic, color 76 (Elm Blue)
A: Ella Rae Classic, color 44 (Yellow)
B: Ella Rae Classic, color 01 (White)

Hoodie Bird Blanket
MC: Berrocco Comfort, color 9735 (Delft Blue)
A: Berrocco Comfort, color 9724 (Pumpkin)
B: Red Heart Classic, color 0001 (White)
C: Red Heart Classic, color 00012 (Black)

Sydney the Snuggly Penguin
MC: Ella Rae Classic, color 32 (Black)
CC: Ella Rae Classic, color 01 (White)
A: Ella Rae Classic, color 27 (Orange)
B: Ella Rae Classic, color 76 (Elm Blue)

Polar Penguin Hat
MC: Red Heart Classic, color 0012 (Black)
CC: Red Heart Classic, color 0001 (White)
A: Berroco Comfort, color 9724 (Pumpkin)
B: Berroco Comfort, color 9735 (Delft Blue)

Timmy the Teddy Bear
MC: Ella Rae Classic, color 17 (Chocolate)
CC: Brown Sheep Nature Spun, color N93W (Latte)

Striped Bear Blanket
MC: Red Heart Designer Sport, color 3201 (Banana Cream)
CC: Red Heart Designer Sport, color 3620 (Celadon)
A: Patons Astra, color 02020 (Medium Tan)
B: Patons Astra, color 02010 (Soft Tan)
C: Patons Astra, color 02013 (Dark Tan)

Hazel the Bouncy Bunny
MC: Ella Rae Classic, color 01 (White)
CC: Ella Rae Classic, color 54 (Bubblegum)

Bunny Rabbit Hat
MC: Red Heart Classic, color 0001 (White)
CC: Red Heart Classic, color 0737 (Pink)
A: Red Heart Classic, color 0012 (Black)
B: Red Heart Classic, color 0818 (Blue Jewel)

Clive the Cuddly Pig
MC: Ella Rae Classic, color 54 (Bubblegum)
CC: Ella Rae Classic, color 32 (Black)

Swirly Pig Blanket
MC: Red Heart Designer Sport, color 3301 (Latte)
CC: Patons Astra, color 02010 (Soft Tan)
A: Red Heart Sport, color 0724 (Baby Pink)
B: Patons Astra, color 02765 (Black)
C: Patons Astra, color 02721 (White)

Kendra the Kitty Cat
MC: Ella Rae Classic, color 122 (Ironside Grey)
CC: Ella Rae Classic, color 54 (Bubblegum)

Kitty Cat Hat
MC: Red Heart Classic, color 0401 (Nickel)
CC: Red Heart Classic, color 0737 (Pink)
A: Red Heart Classic, color 0012 (Black)
B: Red Heart Classic, color 0001 (White)

Ricky the Kutie Koala
MC: Ella Rae Classic, color 123 (Grey Suit)
CC: Ella Rae Classic, color 01 (White)
A: Ella Rae Classic, color 32 (Black)

Scenic Koala Blanket
MC: Patons Astra, color 02753 (Sky)
CC: Patons Astra, color 02020 (Medium Tan)
A: Patons Astra, color 02729 (Silver Grey Mix)
B: Red Heart Sport, color 0406 (Medium Thyme)
C: Patons Astra, color 02765 (Black)
D: Patons Astra, color 02721 (White)

Lacy the Lovable Mouse
MC: Ella Rae Classic, color 123 (Grey Suit)
CC: Ella Rae Classic, color 54 (Bubblegum)

Sneaky Little Mouse Bib
MC: Red Heart Designer Sport, color 3201 (Banana Cream)
A: Patons Astra, color 02729 (Silver Grey Mix)
B: Red Heart Sport color, 0724 (Baby Pink)
C: Patons Astra, color 02765 (Black)

Franklin the Fluffy Sheep
MC: Ella Rae Classic, color 01 (White)
CC: Ella Rae Classic, color 32 (Black)

Chunky Sheep Blanket
MC: Lion Brand Homespun, color 389 (Spring Green)
A: Plymouth Yarn Oh My!, color 9 (White)
B: Bernat Satin, color 04040 (Ebony)

Pete the Plush Pickup Truck
MC: Ella Rae Classic, color 31 (Cherry)
A: Ella Rae Classic, color 32 (Black)
B: Ella Rae Classic, color 44 (Yellow)
C: Ella Rae Classic, color 123 (Grey Suit)

On the Road Pickup Bib
A: Red Heart Designer Sport, color 3620 (Celadon)
B: Patons Astra, color 02729 (Silver Grey Mix)
C: Patons Astra, color 02753 (Sky)
D: Patons Astra, color 02721 (White)
E: N. Y. Cotton, color 10 (Red)
F: Patons Astra, color 02765 (Black)
G: Red Heart Designer Sport, color 3201 (Banana Cream)

Resources

Please contact the following manufacturers to learn where you can purchase their products.

Yarns

Bernat
www.bernat.com
Satin (100% acrylic, 3.5 oz, 163 yards) **4**

Berroco
www.berroco.com
Comfort (50% nylon, 50% acrylic, 3.5 oz, 210 yards) **4**

Brown Sheep
www.brownsheep.com
Nature Spun (100% wool, 3.5 oz, 245 yards) **4**

Coats and Clark
www.coatsandclark.com; www.redheart.com
Red Heart Designer Sport (100% acrylic, 3 oz, 279 yards) **3**
Red Heart Sport (100% acrylic, 2.5 oz, 165 yards) **3**
Red Heart Classic (100% acrylic, 3.5 oz, 190 yards) **4**

Knitting Fever
www.knittingfever.com
Ella Rae Classic (100% wool, 3.5 oz, 219 yards) **4**

Lion Brand
www.lionbrand.com
Homespun (98% acrylic, 2% polyester, 6 oz, 185 yards) **5**

Patons
www.patonsyarns.com
Astra (100% acrylic, 1.75 oz, 161 yards) **3**

Plymouth Yarns
www.plymouthyarn.com
Oh My! (100% nylon, 50 g, 70 yards) **5**

Takhi Stacy Charles
www.nyyarns.com
N. Y. Cotton (100% cotton mercerized, 3.5 oz, 231 yards) **4**

Hooks and Notions

Buttons
www.buttonsetc.com
Adorable children's buttons

Eyes and Noses
Check your local craft supply store, or visit:

ArtCove
www.artcove.com
Eyes and noses

http://teddybearinabox.com
Recordable Voice Inserts

Hooks

Susan Bates
www.coatsandclark.com
Aluminum and plastic crochet hooks

Clover
www.clover-usa.com
Bamboo crochet hooks

Stitch Markers
Clover
www.clover-usa.com
Locking stitch markers

Stuffing
Check your local craft supply store or visit www.joann.com.

Tapestry Needles
Susan Bates
www.coatsandclark.com
Plastic tapestry needles

Bryson Distributing
www.brysonknits.com
Bent-tip and straight metal tapestry needles

Yarn Bobbins
Check your local yarn store or visit:

www.brysonknits.com
Yarn bobbins for color work

About the Author

Stacey Trock was born and raised in Silver Spring, Maryland, where her mom taught her to crochet at the age of six. Although she loved crochet, her pursuit of the craft was limited to entries in the county fair and presents for family.

The summer after finishing school, Stacey was in the midst of a quarter-life crisis, and her boyfriend was away in Europe. Looking for something to do, she designed two crocheted stuffed animals. And she hasn't stopped since! After making her first animals, she heard the call of the crochet bug loud and clear and went into crocheting full-time. In 2008, she founded FreshStitches, an amigurumi design company, where many of her stuffed animal designs are featured.

In addition to designing, she also works at a fantastic yarn store, where she teaches knitting and crochet and also helps customers solve yarn-related crises. In her free time, Stacey loves to travel and, since she isn't looking for a change in vocation any time soon, tries not to get left at home during any more European expeditions.

SEE MORE ONLINE!

a fresh approach to crochet

★ *Visit www.freshstitches.com to view the full range of Stacey's designs.*

★ *Read Stacey's blog at www.freshstitches.com/wordpress.*

★ *Check out www.martingale-pub.com for more fun crochet and knitting books.*